From the Village
to the Ends of the Earth

From the Village to the Ends of the Earth

LIVING AND WORKING WITH
A BIBLELESS PEOPLE
TO BRING THEM THE WORD OF GOD

Lisa Leidenfrost

With illustrations by

Noai Leidenfrost Meyer

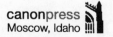
canonpress
Moscow, Idaho

Published by Canon Press
P. O. Box 8729, Moscow, Idaho 83843
800-488-2034 | www.canonpress.com

Library of Congress Cataloging-in-Publication Data

Leidenfrost, Lisa, author.
From the village to the ends of the earth : living and working with
   a bibleless people to bring them the word of God / Lisa Leidenfrost ;
   with illustrations by Noai Leidenfrost Meyer.
Moscow, Idaho : Canon Press, [2021]
LCCN 2020050056 | ISBN 9781947644717 (paperback)
LCSH: Missionaries—Côte d'Ivoire—Biography. |
   Missionaries—United States—Biography.
Classification: LCC BV3625.I82 L45 2021 | DDC 266/.42092 [B]—dc23
LC record available at https://lccn.loc.gov/2020050056

20 21 22 23 24 25 26 27 28 29   10 9 8 7 6 5 4 3 2

CONTENTS

This book is dedicated to my husband and children, who are the main characters in my life, and to the Bakwé people, who are the ones we spent a lifetime bringing the word of God to. Please pray for the Bakwé that they would hear the Word, respond to it, and flood into His kingdom so that the entirety of Bakwéland will shine with God's light and love.

PREFACE

"He shall have dominion also from sea to sea,
and from the River to the ends of the earth."

PSALM 72:8

The work of discipling the nations sometimes means sending missionaries to the uttermost parts of the earth. And bringing God's Word for the first time to an unreached people group is definitely a difficult task. But are missionaries superheroes doing superhuman things—or are they just normal Christians with an extraordinary God? When God calls His children to a hard task, He goes there with them and makes it all possible. But why go to a small village on the other side of the earth when there is so much work still to be done in one's own country? God calls and equips some of His children to go to foreign places because all nations are His and He is spreading His kingdom to the ends of the earth. He is the King of Kings and Lord of Lords, and His people go out in His service.

When God calls a family to live overseas in a village, it also means bringing their children along too. Stories of our family are scattered throughout this book on purpose, because family life is an integral part of the "real work." Raising our children for Christ means pouring into them daily, providing a family life that is both fun and filled with the grace and love of Christ in action. When children grow up to follow the Lord with their whole heart, they are a powerful witness for Christ.

God's kingdom work can be done wherever you are as you walk faithfully with Him, but in this book I focus on what it is like to translate the Bible into an unwritten language, from the start of learning it without any books, to later trying to find just the right words for key biblical concepts that are completely missing in the target language.

Language is also influenced by culture, so one must seek to understand how people view their world as well, and this can mean trying to make sense of a view that is entirely different from one's own. For example, what explanation is given when someone is sick for a prolonged period of time? What importance do dreams and bad thoughts have? What do people fear? All of this helps us understand who they are, so to better know how to reach them for Christ.

At times, missionary life can take twists and turns that are unexpected. Sometimes God calls His people to really difficult things, like getting caught in civil wars. This book gives you an inside view of some challenging situations that missionaries have found themselves in, and how God came through. It shows the hardships and sacrifice that people must be willing to make when they take up a work like this. But it is all a part of the process and privilege of taking part in God's Kingdom work as it spreads from sea to sea and from the River to the ends of the earth.

~Lisa Leidenfrost

CHAPTER ONE

ENTERING THE VILLAGE

"There's the village!" the kids shouted. The sun was setting behind the giant tropical trees in the distance as we entered the sleepy village of Touadji II. It didn't seem possible that we had been gone for an entire year from our home. Yet, it was still the same with its deeply rutted roads worn by the rains. While we drove in past the worn, wooden shops and rounded the corner, we could see the tin-roofed houses slipping into the shadows of the departing sun. Smoke from the kitchen fires wafted through the thatch of the cook houses as women prepared for the evening meal. It all seemed so peaceful and quiet, until our truck was spotted, and the place came to life.

1

Village women with babies on their backs set down their bundles and ran excitedly toward us. Men waved enthusiastically and joined the growing throng. Soon the fading light of the setting sun was totally blocked from our view as white smiling teeth set in dark, shining faces filled the windows. Bakwé children pushed through the adults and extended their little hands to clasp my children's as they greeted them with the typical Bakwé greeting of "Ayo." By now, other people were running up to the truck with exclamations of joy and pleasure in their efforts to welcome us heartily home. Adults, too, thrust their hands in the window to grasp ours in a Bakwé gesture of friendship to reestablish a relationship that had been interrupted for far too long.

After the excitement of greeting this initial group, we drove down the dirt road followed by our escort of village children running behind and came to another series of courtyards. These people ran out to greet us as well in successive waves. When the last group receded from our view, we turned into the dirt road that led to our house where we were met by a wiggling ball of pent up energy, who was barking his joy at our return. We drove around the house to the back, and Janvier, our cook, came running out of the kitchen and gave us an enthusiastic greeting. As the truck was unloaded, Janvier talked non-stop to my husband, Csaba[1], in French. I went into the courtyard and was greeted by

---

1 Csaba is a Hungarian given name pronounced *Chaba*.

my mongoose whistling frantically at the sound of our voices. When I opened her cage and picked her up, she did her routine thing and wet all over my shirt with a nasty smelling liquid which was her unique way of saying "I missed you."

Csaba by now had entered the kitchen with Janvier still talking a mile a minute. When I got in, I showed Janvier a can of sauce that he could add to a can of hotdogs for a quick meal. As Janvier resumed talking to Csaba about the year's events, I slipped out into my garden. Everything was so beautiful! The flowers were in bloom and the grass had started to fill in nicely. I looked around and the emotions of being home filled me with warmth. It had been so long since I had last seen all this. I looked at our fruit trees and was pleased that they were heavily laden with oranges, so I gathered some and headed back into the house. I glanced into the pot that was rapidly boiling on the stove and noticed something funny about the sauce. I didn't pay it too much mind since Janvier is a good, creative cook but still, I wondered.

About now Alexis and Perez, Csaba's translation and literacy coworkers, came to greet us. As they talked in the kitchen, Janvier was setting the table with the sauce placed in the middle. Curious, I picked up the lid and yes, it still looked a bit odd, so I tasted it. Sure enough, my worst suspicions were confirmed. Janvier, in his excitement on seeing us, had opened a can of applesauce by mistake. It was garnished with hotdogs floating in the middle. As I pointed this out, he groaned and said, "Oh, I was just so happy to see you that I wasn't paying attention. I really don't like it when you're away, and there is so much to talk about." (Applesauce with hotdogs wasn't too bad, but I don't recommend it.)

That night after unpacking a few items, we went to the courtyard of Alexis' family and sat for a while shooting the breeze, Bakwé style. One of the wives chatted with me as we sat around a lantern on wooden stools enjoying the evening. It was a comfortable feeling, the feeling of belonging, of seeing familiar faces that care about you. It was the feeling of life going on with you a part of it.

In a strange way we belonged there, and even though we were very different from each other, we had a place in their lives and they in ours. We were home.

THE VILLAGE OF TOUADJI II

We lived in a remote corner of the Ivory Coast about a two-hour drive from the coastal town of San Pédro. If you drove up this road, you would come to the village where we lived. It was not impressive or set apart in any way, except that it was the place we made our home. This village was full of Bakwé, a people who, before our arrival in 1989, had no written language and were largely without the knowledge of God's grace and salvation. You could even say that they were an unreached people group.

This Bakwé village, like the others, was full of mud and stick houses cracked by the sun's baking and worn with time. There was also an occasional concrete house scattered amongst the earthen ones. No matter how prosperous or how poor, the houses were all surrounded by a network of dirt paths that were the stomping grounds of goats, chickens, ducks, guinea fowl, pigs, and sheep which always seemed to be where you wished they were not. These roads were also filled with children playing, women going to market bearing heavy loads on their heads, men going off to their fields—by people, in general, living out their daily lives.

If you looked beyond all this, our house was in the farthest corner of the village on the edge between civilization and the wilds beyond. This wilderness kept encroaching upon us with its unwanted creatures that had a nasty habit of visiting us at night. We had cobras and driver ants drop in from time to time and even an elusive crocodile that decided to take up its residence in one of our murky ponds. Unlike the wilderness beyond our borders, our property was filled with flowers, fruit trees and carpeted with thick grass—a veritable Garden of Eden.

In this lush corner, on the edge of the village, Csaba translated the Bible with his team while I taught our four children, Hans, Noai (only daughter), Andreas, and Jeremiah. We didn't have many modern conveniences, but we were happy, with our dog, two cats, two mongooses, various chickens, several ducks, and a sassy parrot. Here is a look into our lives and the process it takes to bring the Bible to a Bibleless people who have never had a written language before, and also what it is like for an American family to live in a place so very different from our own homeland. These are stories and sketches taken from different periods, that culminate in the end, with the rumblings of a civil war.

GOD HAS NOT FORGOTTEN US

Upon first entering Bakwé land for an initial visit in 1989, Csaba did a survey to find out if there were any Christians amongst the Bakwé. He had spent days traveling with a fellow missionary, visiting villages and asking if there were any Bakwé who considered themselves Christians. Each time the answer he received was no. He then visited existing churches that were led by other ethnic peoples in the nearby towns, asking the same question and getting the same response. He wondered if there were any Christians at all amongst the Bakwé or were these people completely unreached for Christ?

After this survey trip, we moved as a family to the town of Soubré, situated on the fringe of Bakwé territory, where we rented a house from the Christian Missionary Alliance (CMA) mission. We had two children at the time, a two-year-old and a baby. From our rented home, Csaba went into Bakwé territory again and did a language survey, this time to determine which village had the most central dialect to use for the translation and also which was the most prestigious of them all. This would be the one that all the different dialects could understand and would be recognized as the original Bakwé. After analyzing the results, he picked the village of Touadji II. When we got approval from the village elders and were given a piece of land, Csaba took daily trips to build our home. While in Soubré, we visited different local churches still trying to find out if there were any Bakwé believers.

During one of these Sunday visits, Csaba got up during the announcements and explained that we had come to translate God's Word into the Bakwé language and were there any Bakwé in the congregation? Before he finished speaking, two older Bakwé women shot up in joyful exuberance and started to dance in circles and sing. They were deeply moved and praised

God over and over in their song as they danced. Then the women stopped dancing and said, "God has heard our prayer. We have been praying for many years that He would send someone to the Bakwé. Now they have come. God has not forgotten the Bakwé!"

We were thrilled. We now found two evangelical believers out of ten thousand or more people and we were evidently an answer to their prayers! Later we visited another evangelical church in town to see if there were any more and found five Bakwé young men who had been evangelized at one of the church's outreaches. Somehow these men happened to be in the right place at the right time, and God touched their hearts to grant them His salvation. Csaba began meeting with these young men and encouraged them to think about starting a branch of the church amongst their own people. They took up the suggestion and started one in the village of Galéa which was the very first Bakwé Protestant church that we knew of.

Soon the Bakwé started to come to that church and we worshiped with them to encourage them. Having a toddler and baby in tow came with its own challenges. The church met in a small mud and thatch meeting hall, where it became unbearably hot as people crowded into the tightly packed space. On top of that, no one ever knew how many hours the service would last. This was hard for very young children.

On one hot Sunday, partway into the sermon, one or both of my kids had gotten fussy and started to cry.

They were hot, miserable, and it wasn't to their liking, so I took them out of the service.

Once out in the blazing tropical sun, we were surrounded by a wall of curious onlookers who wanted to stare at the white people. I guess we were a rarity in those parts. To get away from the wall of onlookers and out of the air-stagnation zone, I took the kids to the truck that was now baked from the sun. We got inside and opened some windows to let in a little breeze which started to cool down the oven. But not for long, because the onlookers had caught up with us and were blocking all the windows. They evidently were not done with their show and we were the main attraction. On top of being surrounded by watchful eyes, the children were hungry and started to fuss some more, since it was now past noon.

I could still hear the preacher in the background thundering out his sermon and it didn't sound like he was about to end any time soon. I tried to keep the kids happy the best I could in the stifling heat with our wall of attentive onlookers. When the service finally ended, people wanted to greet Csaba and talk with him, which was really important in Africa. By the time he arrived back at the truck and saw the state of the children, he realized something needed to change. So we had to get creative to make it work for the kids. I forget exactly how we did it, and it was never easy, but we managed somehow with snacks and fans and things to do. We then went back Sunday after Sunday to encourage the young fledgling church. And, thankfully, after a while, when the kids and I routinely left the service, our throng of viewers got less and less as they became more accustomed to us. But, I noticed, we were never left entirely alone.

THE PROPHET HARRIS

Csaba researched the history of our area and found that there were numerous Harrist churches already in the Bakwé territory. These were independent African churches and had been influenced by William Wadé Harris (often referred to as the Prophet Harris).

In 1913, William Wadé Harris came walking barefoot along the coast from Liberia into Ivory Coast. He wore a long, white robe that had black sashes crisscrossed around his chest and he held a staff in his hand. He went from village to village allegedly doing miracles and telling people to burn their fetishes and turn to God. Many people did. He taught the ten commandments, and had his followers worship on Sunday. Aside from teaching them songs using their own style of music, Harris also told them to wait for the white man who would bring them the Bible. He said that if a man came who did not have the Bible, he was a lying man and they were not to listen to him. He also said that one day the white man and the black man would sit down at the same table to eat together. People considered this last saying a prophecy. Because of the Prophet Harris, many regions were ripe for missionaries who came after him. Not long after there were many established protestant churches of different denominations in other language groups. Not only that, but an indigenous church called the Harrist Church also took root along large portions of the Ivory Coast.

As the legend goes, when the prophet came to our general region, the people rejected him, so he put a curse on the whole area and said that they would be overlooked by development. This proved to be true. But in the 1960s the Bakwé finally turned and joined the Harrist religion, setting up churches in every village and installing Harrist priests. Yet in most cases the priests did not know how to read, and the Bible in the French language remained a closed book. The concepts of grace and the gospel were little understood because there was no Bible in their language and they had limited access to those who could teach them.

The Harrists in our area did not consider themselves connected with the Protestant churches in any way and shunned them; hence when we asked if there were any Christians, they assumed we meant only Protestants. They would say that they were "Harrist" and not "Protestant." They had a basic belief in God but had an incomplete understanding of the Scriptures. The Harrist churches at that time had their own forms and rituals mixed in with some of their pagan beliefs and their lives were little changed after becoming Harrist. Yet when the church bell tolled at four o'clock a.m. people would file into the church to sing and chant as part of their daily ritual. That was what we found when we entered Bakwé land in 1989. Our goal was to get the scriptures into their hands so that they could have a full knowledge of the gospel and why Jesus came to this earth to die for us.

GETTING AROUND IN TOWN

Getting around town and doing the shopping was always an interesting experience. Shopping was usually not a simple matter of walking into a store and paying the price listed on the tag, since one had to play the market game first.

On one such day when Csaba was in town, a stranger called out from inside a booth laden with goods, "Hey mustache! My friend. I haven't seen you in a long, long while. Where have you been? I've got a good price for you today since you are my very good friend. Come and take a look."

Csaba bent over and picked up an item. His supposed good friend said, "I will give you this item real cheap, especially for you. Normally the price is much higher but since you have come to see me, it is only 2,000 cfa."[2] Csaba responded casually, "But a friend of mine bought one at another booth for much less." The vendor shrugged this new bit of information off and responded, "No, 2,000 cfa is a good price and my quality

2 2,000 cfa is roughly $4.00.

is better. You will not find quality like this. I have this special price only for you."

A very long and drawn-out conversation ensued bartering the price down. Eventually the final cost was decided upon, but not before Csaba's "friend" had given him the runaround with the price. That is just part of the market game.

The vendors in booths can be hard enough to deal with, but the top of my list for hassling were the walking street vendors, who were a very tenacious group of passionate sellers. You didn't have to try and find them: they found you. They spoke a different language and a "No, thank you," in their vendor mind meant "Yes, I want that very much, thank you, but I'm playing hard to get." Even after a hard and firm no, they could still be very difficult to shake off, even following you down the street.

One day while in town, I was latched onto by a street vendor carrying a variety of watches and he was very determined to sell me a bunch of them. I never even spoke much, but only gave a polite nod and a "No, thank you" to discourage him. He didn't take the hint and proceeded to tell me why I needed another watch or two or three. When I didn't exactly specify how many watches I wanted after his appeal, he started shoving a few in my arms. I responded by shoving them back, but he wouldn't take them! This little routine kept up for several more blocks with me still carrying his watches! I

was finally able to give them all back after I somehow convinced his vendor brain that I really did not
need or want his wares. He then left to go harass
another victim. After he was gone and peace ensued,
I asked Csaba what I had done wrong. He simply

said that I had acknowledged the vendor's existence.

LANGUAGE-LEARNING IN THE VILLAGE

After Csaba finished building our house, we thankfully moved from Soubré to Touadji II and settled into life in the village. Csaba's next task was trying to learn the language well enough to pass a language proficiency test which would allow him to move on to the next stage of the work.

Learning a language without books or even an alphabet is a challenge. When we arrived, the Bakwé only spoke their language, so there were no books to guide us. In our linguistic training we were taught how to listen and carefully write down the sounds the human mouth can make using the International Phonetic Alphabet (IPA). We were then taught how to distinguish between those sounds by their point of articulation in the mouth.

To attack the daunting task of learning Bakwé, Csaba first found someone who spoke some French and was willing to help him with language learning. Csaba met with this man often and elicited basic phrases like, "Hello. What is your name?" "Hi, how are you?" "How is your wife/husband?" He recorded these on cassette tape and played them over and over again, trying to mimic the exact intonation. After this, he went out and used these phrases in the village to see how close he was on the pronunciation. The villagers were delighted with this but would inevitably ask, "What are you doing?" Csaba wanted to tell them that he was learning their language but didn't know how to say that phrase in Bakwé yet. So the next day he asked his language helper how to say this. The language helper responded back, "There is not a phrase for this since we don't go around telling each other that we're learning our own language. When they ask you what you are doing, just say, 'I am strolling.'"

That was easy enough, so Csaba got the phrase recorded and memorized. The next day he went around the village using his new phrase, but on hearing it, people broke out laughing. Maybe his language helper was playing a practical joke on him? Someone eventually pulled him aside and said that he was really telling everyone that he was sleeping. Csaba discovered that Bakwé was a tonal language and changing the tone just slightly changed the whole meaning of the phrase.

To help him learn the language and integrate into Bakwé society he also spent a lot of time being around people by eating with them, going to their farms, or just hanging out under the shade of a tree chatting. One day Csaba really got the conversation going without meaning to. He was sitting under a tree with a bunch of older men in the heat of the day. They were engaging in light conversation, the type one does when little effort is required or thought wanted. To take part in it, Csaba mentioned casually that my dad just had open-heart surgery. Like pouring gasoline on an ember that quickly shot into flame, the group shot to attention and responded with the Bakwé expression of incredulity, "Yeeeeeeeeee!" How could this be? Immediately all eyes turned to Csaba for an explanation. Csaba went on to tell them how the doctors opened up my dad's chest to work on his heart.

A Bakwé man said, "How do they do that? Do they take a machete and whack at him?"

An older man beside him answered, "No, they have to do it gently or they'll kill the guy."

The first man mused, "Wow, imagine opening up someone's chest!"

A third man shook his head, "Yup, these white men can do anything now."

Csaba then explained how they performed open-heart surgeries in Abidjan too with African doctors trained in France.

They were amazed. "Imagine, opening up someone's chest to expose the heart. Why, we just die here in the village!"

⋈⊕⋊

While learning the language, Csaba had to establish what consonants and vowels Bakwé really had. He wrote down the phrases he heard then analyzed the breakdown of the letters. If he found two words that had everything the same about them except for the first consonant, then that proved the consonants were true and not conditioned by the environment of the letters around them. This is called a minimal pair. An example in English would be *pan* and *ban*. This is done with vowels too, like *pin* and *pan* where the *i* and *a* are true and not conditioned by their environment. In this way he could find the true letters for the alphabet. Sometimes he found a consonant that was especially difficult to decipher. In one of those times, he had a young man volunteer to help. Csaba sprayed his mouth with powdered charcoal, then had him say the word. With a flashlight Csaba looked in his mouth and saw where the tongue hit the roof of the mouth to show exactly which consonant was being spoken.

Consonants were one thing, but distinguishing vowels was a completely different one. Bakwé unfortunately had central unrounded vowels which were indistinguishable to our western ears, yet so distinct to a Bakwé's. In our training we were told that central vowels were hard to tell apart but not to worry since it was very rare to have one language that had them all. Well it turned out that Bakwé was one of those rare languages. They had thirteen distinct vowels which made hearing the difference between them very difficult. To find out just how many vowels were actually there, Csaba had to do a frequency analysis by using a spectrogram which analyzed the sound frequency to determine the difference between the central back vowels. This way he could discover if they were all true vowels or just derivations of each other.

After he got his vowels and consonants written down, he had to discover if there were rules that governed the complicated sound system before he could isolate the minimal number of vowels and consonants needed to form the alphabet. He had to decipher what sounds were true letters and not conditioned by the consonants or vowels they were next to. If they were conditioned in any way, then they were not true letters but changed only upon the condition. For example, a normal vowel can turn to a nasalized vowel in the presence of a nasalized consonant like an *m* or an *n*. This does not make it a new vowel but only one that can be conditioned by its environment, so it would not be added to the alphabet.

Besides the consonants and vowels, Csaba had fun figuring out how many tones Bakwé had. He initially thought there were four or five tones, but some ended up being conditioned by their surroundings again, which made them not true tones. After much study, he settled on just three tones: high, mid, and low, with combinations of those tones across syllables of words. In a tonal language a slight shift in tone changes the meaning of the word completely. We decided to write the tone on the initial syllable of Bakwé words. For example, a high tone over the word *na,* means *my,* and a low tone over the same word means *your,* so getting the tones right was crucial. One time, Csaba got the tone wrong and introduced me to a chief, saying "This is your wife."

After this, he analyzed and then worked on the grammar, based upon his collection of texts. He looked at the patterns of subject, object, and verb placement which was different from our own language. He noticed that when verb auxiliaries were used in negation, the verb jumped to the very end of the sentence. So a Bakwé phrase like "He loves me" switches to "He not me loves" when in the negative. The whole process of analyzing the language was fascinating because he was being a language detective trying to find clues and solve challenging grammar mysteries. Yes, Bakwé was a difficult language, and we wished we had some books to explain it all to us, but we were making those books, and that took time.

CHAPTER TWO

SCHOOL

While Csaba analyzed the language, I kept up with our children and the house which was a full-time job that I wanted to do well. On the side I learned as much of the language as I could through a tutor. Then, over the next several years, my job increased when we added two more children to our family to equal four. While still trying to keep up with some language learning myself, I spent most of my time running the house and schooling the kids, which was a challenge living where we did. It was fun to teach children who wanted to learn, especially if those children were your own. But I still welcomed help, and it came to us one day out of the blue.

We were told that Susan, a new schoolteacher, had some extra time before going up to teach the Saunders children, whose parents, Philip and Heather, were doing translation work just north of us. We were happy to have her come to our village and teach for a couple weeks, since teachers showing up to help were few and far between.

She was young and wanted to get in a little overseas teaching experience before she started her own career as a teacher. Through correspondence, we found out that she did not like creepy crawlies too well. (We all have our faults.) Unfortunately, we had lots of what she didn't like in our house and all over our property. But to be good hosts, we decided to rid the place of creepy crawlies the best we could. I was pleased with the success of our first eradication efforts. I thought she would be too, but her initial reaction proved otherwise.

Since all of our bedrooms were occupied by kids at the time, we sectioned off a room for her in the dining area by hanging a large mat from the ceiling. We placed a bed and table in it with a kerosene lamp. I thought it quite nice.

When I showed her the room, I mentioned proudly, "We just killed a family of rats in the mat ceiling above your space. I think they're all dead now. We fed them to the cats. Oh, by the way, there still are quite a few mice, but we consider them permanent residents. Don't let them bother you. They stay pretty much in the thatch until night."

I thought she would be pleased with this information, but she was strangely quiet. Then to make conversation, she asked me why we had a bamboo fence around our place. I casually mentioned that we put that up to protect us from the rabid dogs that were prevalent during this time of year. Again—silence. I had this uneasy feeling that we were striking out.

Before she went to bed, I felt it was only fair to warn her about the driver ant raids that periodically ended up in our yard. On rare occasions they even found their way into the kitchen for a midnight snack. When they came in, they ate everything, even the soap. She asked if they bite and I said, "My, do they bite! They can de-flesh a live chicken and leave only the bones! But it's OK, we left a kerosene lamp by your bed so that you can check the floor before you get out of bed at night because there's nothing worse than having the army crawl up your legs to do battle."

At this point she was visibly concerned so I quickly reassured her by adding, "The ants aren't all that bad, when they come, they pretty much keep the snakes away."

"Snakes!?" she responded with alarm.

"Why yes, just last week our worker chased a black cobra into the bush. Too bad he got away."

Again, silence until it was broken with, "Uh, when did you say that bus left for the city?"

That was just a mild threat. But I really thought we would lose her after the spider incident. One night I heard a shriek coming from the living room, so I ran in there to find her pointing uneasily at the wall. I looked up and saw the biggest wall spider I had seen in our house in a long time.

"Wow," I exclaimed excitedly, "That one's a beauty! Hey, Csaba, help me to get this one as a specimen for Gordon, the science prof. We can send it back when . . ." *Whack!* "Oops, missed. Oh well, maybe he will surface again sometime later."

After all, we were Wildlife Management graduates and we had a hobby of collecting the local creepy crawlies. Unfortunately, our new teacher didn't share our hobby. I looked over at her to see how she was enjoying this new excitement and found her clutching her knees tightly against her chest with her feet tucked neatly underneath, out of harm's way.

"It's all right," I comforted her, "They don't bite that I know of and they're all over the house. You'll get used to them."

I then went to take my bucket shower and get ready for bed. As I came back through the living room to turn off the lantern, I was surprised to find her much in the same position as before with her knees clutched tightly to her chest. I suggested that she go to bed. As I left the living room, I shook my head, wondering if she was going to make it.

She taught the kids the first few days and did a wonderful job. The city bus had come and gone, and she was not on it. So far so good. Still trying to redeem our rough start, I decided to show her the countryside, since it was quite charming. That afternoon, Csaba drove us to our friend's cocoa farm. We started walking down the path of the cocoa forest, when I noticed that she had not followed me because she was afraid of those dreaded snakes. I came back and reassured her that if she followed behind me, the snakes would get me first—she need have no worries. She seemed satisfied with this and followed. As we were enjoying our walk through the shaded cocoa forest on that beautiful sunny day, I looked behind and noticed her bending over something. On closer inspection I found it to be one of those giant African millipedes. "Don't touch those," I warned. "They say that the bite will leave a nasty burn." She backed away and seemed relieved that there was finally something that crawled, that was not in our house. We continued our walk.

Later that night, as we both went into the kitchen to get some water, I nearly stumbled over one of those giant millipedes. Quicker than lightning, and before she saw what I was doing, I shot that thing out the door and into the yard like a little brown hockey puck. Luckily, she didn't see that silent maneuver. The less house wildlife she saw, the better.

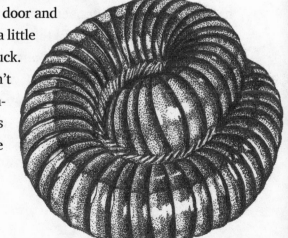

One thing that was going in our favor was that she liked our parrot. But honestly, I don't know why, because whatever he kept garbling about, in the tone that he sometimes said it in, I can imagine it was enough to cause the hair to fly off a wart hog. Even so, she liked the parrot and our kids, the two redeeming factors.

I thought that a look around our quaint village with the friendly people would do her good as well. We walked into the village and upon entering a courtyard, I noticed that the atmosphere was unusually charged. Angry words were flying above us in a major war of verbal abuse with the next courtyard. I could see I had struck out again. "Yes, this is our village. Like it?"

I can't say we scored many points on the village outing or the field outing, or at our home and surroundings, but she still liked the kids and had not left us yet. She ended up staying her full allotted time and did a splendid job with the teaching and was much appreciated. I was also relieved to hear that she would be prepared to come back if it worked out in her schedule. She was a tough woman and if this was what she had to go through to get her overseas experience, then she deserved a medal. Thankfully none of our resident snakes decided to make an appearance during her stay. Otherwise I had the feeling that we would be out of luck for the future. After she left, we found a tarantula and a snake in the house. But we won't tell her that, will we?

Postscript: Wycliffe will send people for various short-term projects to help those on the field. The people sent to us have been a wonderful addition and help. One brilliant short-termer, John Longley, helped Csaba with the initial Bakwé grammar analysis and saved Csaba about two years of work.

And concerning our home, through the years we made improvements on the house by patching the cracks under the doors that kept out all the snakes, all lizards, most ant raids, most rat encounters, but not the mice. Some things you just can't get rid of no matter how hard you try. The spiders and geckos were still permanent residents, but we didn't mind them. They always added that special touch to the décor.

CHAPTER THREE

THE GUESTS

In seeking to be accepted by the villagers, hospitality was another important part of the culture that we engaged in when we could. But it was sometimes fraught with surprises, and I often felt unprepared when we invited guests to eat. What did hospitality look like in the village? It had been our experience that when we invited five people, ten could come. We might invite them for noon, but they'd show up at three since time didn't have the same meaning. If they didn't show up at three, then we might have to go looking for them to remind them to come. When they came, they might not know when to leave. They could be there for the rest of the day or evening. You just never knew. But that was village hospitality for you.

I looked out the kitchen door and was amazed because I saw twelve men arriving for dinner. I said to Janvier, "Ok, that's two more than expected. Put on some additional plates." Janvier dutifully put on two more plates. A little time passed and five more walked down our sandy driveway. I called out to Janvier, "Add five more!"

I heard a scuffling in the kitchen and knew my orders were being carried out. In the meantime, Csaba and I were greeting men, welcoming them into the dining room off the kitchen. The dining room was quickly filling up with Bakwé men, much more than we had expected. There was a lag time when three more stragglers came wanting to join the party. Janvier bustled around adding more plates. The room was now full, and we were ready to begin even though we had now doubled the guest list.

We had asked the chief who should be invited, and he gave us a list of ten men but twenty were now there. No matter, we just sat them down at two long tables made of boards slapped over sawhorses. These were adorned with bright patterned cloths with a bottle of coke at each place, after our yard worker had dashed off to get some more. Janvier, being African, had cooked a feast knowing what would happen to the numbers, and there was enough.

Csaba said a prayer and then Janvier passed the rice down the first row of men. Each man heaped rice high on his plate as the bowl went down the tables. They then waited expectantly for the main attraction. This came in the form of a beef dish which was passed down the line of hungry men. They liberally applied the meat to their rice. When a different dish of chicken and sauce came around, they garnished the rice even more. When a third dish arrived, this proved problematic since there was no more room on their plate. But the food still kept coming so they stuck some of the meat in their pockets, thinking of their families at home. (In Bakwé society, back then, the men ate separately.) The men ate meat and relished it. They ate chicken, chewed the bones sucking the delicious marrow, then spat the remainder on the floor. They talked, joked, and laughed through it all.

Then came the dessert of chocolate cake. Normally there is no dessert in a Bakwé meal except for peeled oranges for special occasions, so this was a novelty. What was also a novelty was that we served chocolate cake to the very men who grew the cocoa beans themselves, since Ivory Coast is one of the world's largest cocoa producers. One fellow, after tasting the cake said, "Aha! So, this is how our cocoa beans are being used. This is so good! Why don't we do this?"

So, they ate cake and stuck it in their pockets and drank Coke while jokes were made, and laughter rang around the table. Everyone had a great time. They thanked us profusely and left without leaving a crumb behind them literally, as the leftovers went home in their pockets.

CHAPTER FOUR

CHURCH

When we first arrived in our village, there was not a Bakwé church there. The first church that was started while we were in Soubré was over an hour's drive away, which was too far for most people to attend. As the Bakwé slowly converted to Christianity, some of the Christians gravitated to the already existing churches in the area that were led by other ethnic groups. In our earlier years, Csaba had a habit of visiting these churches because he wanted to see where the Bakwé were going to church so that our translation could be used in each place. It was fun to visit them to experience the different customs of each, and some of those customs were pretty different from what we were used to.

For example, every church had its own unique style of keeping people awake. In one church, while Csaba was sitting quietly, listening to a long sermon on a hot day, the preacher stamped his foot and the whole congregation shot up out of their seats to attention. Csaba scrambled up too or he would have been left alone on the bench. This was repeated throughout the sermon at unpredictable moments. He found out later that if the preacher thought the attention was waning, he would stamp his foot to find out who was truly asleep since they would be the only ones left sitting on the bench. These were awakened to the amusement of all. You never knew when the stamp would come so you had to pay pretty close attention.

In other churches, a monitor walked the aisles with a long stick. If someone fell asleep, the monitor leaned over and poked the sleeper awake. Some older folks had to be poked many times before they came out of their slumber. One older man was poked repeatedly with no success when he started to argue angrily with the monitor in his sleep.

A more common way to see if people were awake was to shout out "Amen!" This was done during the sermon at unpredictable intervals. Amen really meant, "Are you with me?" This was the cue for the whole congregation to shout back, "Hallelujah!" which translated to, "Yes we are, brother, preach it!" If a hearty "Amen" rang out with no subsequent "Hallelujah" then the preacher knew that he'd lost his audience and had better start the closing prayer.

But the best thing to do was to start a church specifically for the Bakwé in our village. Csaba didn't have time to do this in a busy translation schedule. But thankfully, a small church was started in our village by another mission. That mission soon left after a year or so. Csaba then took up the job of encouraging the Bakwé leaders, who at first were his Bakwé coworkers, Firmain and Alexis, until an outside pastor came and took over. We watched the church come to birth and then we watched it struggle and grow. And we attended that church all the time we were in the village. Here is a look into a service.

We walked to church down a little dirt path that was scattered with weeds and deeply rutted from the tropical rains. The sun was already hot at eight a.m., and we could feel the sweat bead up on our necks. We soon entered the churchyard and saw the bent figure of Piguay. She shuffled over to greet us with a smile on her wrinkled face, then turned to go into the church. We filed in behind her to the Leidenfrost family wooden bench, a bench that had been liberally coated with fine silt. We stood waiting for the benches to be wiped, and greeted other people as they went past us to their favorite places.

A little boy with a pair of faded shorts and a ripped T-shirt padded softly by to take his preferred spot on the side bench, near the wall. On, under and around this bench were drums of various sizes and shapes. The only thing that the drums had in common was that none of them worked. He liked this spot and he looked very much like a sentinel of the official drum graveyard.

Then Yaou, ten years old, came boisterously in and beamed a smile at us. He sat down with the rest until he was quickly escorted by a self-appointed usher to the farthest bench at the back wall. From long experience, everyone had learned that Yaou had trouble being quiet. He spoke when he shouldn't, he stood when everyone else was seated, and he could make a general disturbance when he wanted to. He didn't mean to, it just sort of happened, every Sunday. After being shown to his place, he took his post reluctantly as guardian of the back door.

My attention then shifted to the front when Alexis started playing his drum and Firmain sang out the first Bakwé song. The little congregation chimed in with a hearty response. Alexis, an expert and powerful drummer, beat the drum with such force that the vibrations bounced off the bare brick walls and thundered around the room. His drum seemed to reel and shake with the impact, and I could see that this too was destined soon to take its spot at the side, with the boy, in the drum graveyard.

Firmain, the caller, sang out in Bakwé, "If you want to praise God then bring your liver." The congregation responded back, "Don't leave your liver at home".

This went on for about twenty strains with the same thing being said over and over with only a few variations. By the end of the song, we had it memorized. I'm not sure why the same line was repeated so much, but that was the Bakwé way.

Next the announcements were made, and the new arrivals honored. There were no newcomers this week, nor had there been for a long time, but this little routine was kept up in hopes that one day there would be. I looked around at this small congregation of about twenty. They were pretty faithful. I could see nursing moms with their babies sucking away. The row behind them had faithful Yawa, the older man who sat in a bench by himself. In front of the nursing moms were a couple of other men plus Alexis, the drummer. Behind us were the giggling teenage girls. To our left was old

Piguay who sat quietly and attentively when she was not reprimanding the noisy ones seated near her.

Sophie got up and chanted the lead for the next song. Everyone sang the response as the drums thundered the rhythm. Sophie continued to repeat the call while her soft-haired newborn bobbed gently on her back to the beat. Yaou was in the back dancing up a storm which made the teenage girls giggle. They stopped when old Piguay shot them a reprimanding look as someone went to calm the exuberant Yaou down. After several songs of repeating this call/response phrase over and over, we all sat down.

A shy little girl with a soft smile took up an offering stick with a cloth pocket on one end. She wove in and out of the rows of people holding out the stick in front of her to collect any coin that would be put in the offering. When she got to the empty benches, she continued to hold the stick out to those benches too as if there were people in it. Maybe someday there would be.

Prayer was given, and after the sick were prayed for, the sermon began. Firmain opened the French Bible and read a passage from it. This was translated into Bakwé. Then he asked someone else to read the same thing over again in another translation of French. He expounded on it in Bakwé. I'm not sure why they had to read both translations of French, but they felt it was necessary. The time would come soon enough that they would have the Bible in their own language but that was still years in the making. After the final prayer was said, we all stood and greeted each other, and then left for home.

(The first half of the book of Mark was completed later in 1999. The second half in 2002. This gospel was then printed in booklet form so that the people would have something to use while the rest of the New Testament was being translated.)

CHAPTER FIVE

THE LITERACY WORKSHOP

After Csaba was able to reduce the Bakwé language to writing, he began thinking about doing literacy, which was an important step for people to read the Bible when it was completed. He now had a team of three people, Alexis, Perez and Firmain. The first step was for the team to develop primers to teach people how to read and write in Bakwé. After that, they would start up classes. Once the people learned to read, they then needed material to read. Since the language had just been written down, there weren't any booklets available yet. Over time the team would be making booklets on topics that included health, folk tales, short stories and Bible background. In the meantime, to get ready for making the first primer, the team gathered stories of folk tales to get texts to work with. In one of them it explains why the lizard bobs its head, with the moral of the story being that gossip can get you in trouble.

After they got their material, Csaba signed up for a literacy workshop in Bouaké where our other center was located. This was the place where he would be attending workshops over the years on how to tackle different aspects of the translation.

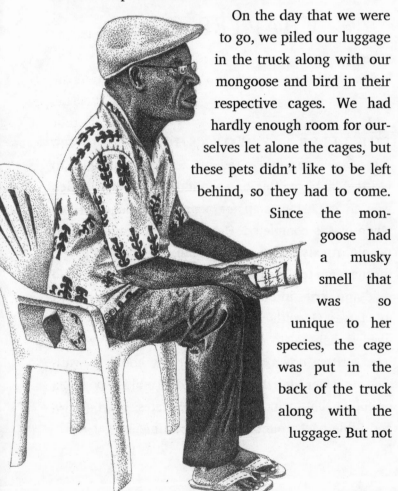

On the day that we were to go, we piled our luggage in the truck along with our mongoose and bird in their respective cages. We had hardly enough room for ourselves let alone the cages, but these pets didn't like to be left behind, so they had to come. Since the mongoose had a musky smell that was so unique to her species, the cage was put in the back of the truck along with the luggage. But not the parrot, as His Royal Highness got to ride with the kids in the back seat.

Once at the center, we settled in the furthest house in the corner of the compound. This was the old manager's house that was no longer in use. We liked it there since it had enough room for our family, plus a large porch that we could use for schooling. This was also the place we put the cages.

When the workshop started, Csaba and the team attended classes on how to make a primer. The first assignment for the team was to determine the frequency of Bakwé letters in a natural text. So, they analyzed the folktales they had transcribed, and found that the letter *a* was used the most frequently, followed by the letters *b, p* and *t.* They needed to use only these four letters in the first lesson, so they had to come up with a short story to practice the letters. Not being able to use any other letters limited the scope of the early lessons. Trying to get an understandable sentence without being ridiculous caused a lot of hilarity in the process. I knew this because I walked into a session and found them nearly rolling on the floor in laughter. But after some effort, they were able to come up with sentences and stories that actually made sense like, "*Ba* (person's name) *pa* (throws) *tata* (a fish net)."

After the primers were put together, they went on to make a teacher's guide. Then, when they got back to the village, they would train teachers on how to use the primer, and send them out to start classes.

THAT
ELUSIVE
MONGOOSE

While Csaba and the team were having fun working on their primer, I was home-schooling the kids on the porch. Our mongoose, affectionately named Goose, did not like her cage and kept asking to be let out. When I did not let her out, I was surprised that she could let herself out. I was in the living room working on math charts one day, when I heard a rustling and a crash. I quickly got up and peeked through the window of the porch, and there was my mongoose on the school table having the time of her life. Instead of plopping her back in her cage, I decided to wait and see what she was capable of doing.

This is what I saw: She walked to a glass of water and pushed it over with her nose spilling the water on the table. She waddled through this mess leaving a trail behind her. She found a crayon box, jumped in and started spewing the crayons in all directions by hiking them between her back legs. She left the box and went over to Andreas' cap gun, stuck her long nose in the barrel and pushed it off the table, and then looked over the side as it fell to the floor. She waddled through some papers, messing them up in the process. After this, she found more toys and pushed them over the edge as well, watching as they hit the ground. To relax, she lay down on a page of homework, and then left her signature mongoose aroma behind in the damp patch left by her wet fur. At this point, I decided to make my entrance before any more damage was done. When I entered the porch, she took one look at me, and then bounded off the table, whistling nervously as she dashed into the drum on the floor. Knowing how hard it was to get her out of the drum, I left her there, hoping she would vacate it before Csaba came home and played. Because, if she was still there when he came to play, he would find the drums strangely muffled before an excited mongoose dashed out. It had happened before. Mongooses messing up the school table was only part of my troubles. Mongooses escaping out of the house altogether was another, because she had learned how to open the porch door by bumping it with her nose, then clawing it open to slip outside.

I learned this new feat of hers, when we were in the cafeteria one morning eating breakfast, and I saw something dark slinking in by the far door. On closer inspection I discovered it was my mongoose who was whistling nervously and coming my way. I guess she didn't want to miss out on breakfast and had come to find us. But, since mongooses in the cafeteria were not very hygienic, we began to lock the porch door. This didn't stop her; it only slowed her down. If she couldn't go out the front, she would let herself out the back. We had lost her so many times that we had many routine frantic searches looking for our elusive mongoose. She would reappear in the oddest places too, like the janitor's closet or back behind the cafeteria where the workers congregated.

To solve the problem of my wandering mongoose, I decided to let her out in the yard but make her real conspicuous, by attaching a hot pink jump rope to her halter with a little green bucket on the other end. The idea of the bucket was to keep her from going anywhere too quickly and it could also be easily spotted bumping along in the grass. She seemed to like the arrangement, and I watched as she went off in the yard lugging her green bucket behind searching for grubs. Satisfied, I went back into the house to finish my work.

I went out later to check on her but couldn't find her anywhere. I asked Csaba if he had seen her, and he told me that she had visited them, but had taken off soon after. I walked around looking for my elusive mongoose wondering where she would turn up next. But instead of seeing a mongoose, I spied only her bucket dangling from a large bush. That was odd, so I walked over and on closer inspection found my mongoose dangling from the other end. There she was, just twirling peacefully in the air suspended by her halter. From the look of things, I guessed she had decided to climb the bush and the bucket wasn't cooperating, so she went back down the other way and just got hung up. I got her out of her predicament and took her back to the house. She would just have to finish the day in her cage, if she would only stay there.

While my mongoose was making adjustments to life in this new place, my kids were also going through their adjustments as well to a much tamer world. At the center, there was not much to do for kids who were used to five acres of wild excitement. The center had some trees, yet the kids had already climbed most of the climbable ones in the walled-in compound and were looking for something else to do. I guess it was not unusual to see one of my boys hanging upside down in a flowered tree where the translators worked in those well-maintained little huts surrounded by sterile decorative bushes. What they needed was something wild to conquer. The only thing that was wild about our center was the thick tangle of bougainvillea hedges adorning the inside of the walls that surrounded the place. So that was where they went, with Hans leading as usual.

The hedge was really just a splash of color cascading down in an impenetrable mass from a ten-foot wall. There was a world behind that hedge and my kids discovered it, then conquered it. It was a world of chambers and passages, rooms and lookouts. I didn't know about this at first, but I did notice that my children would disappear from time to time, without a trace. Then I was invited in, and what I saw was amazing.

Hans, with Noai and Andreas behind, led me through a hole in the hedge into what the kids called The North Gate. I first had to make sure no one was looking, as it would be pretty hard to explain my odd behavior to the African workers (or anyone else for that matter), since going through bushes was not acceptable adult behavior here. Once in, I noticed that the hedge formed a tangle of branches that arched out away from the wall a good six feet. It was clear underneath, yet we were totally hidden. From the outside it looked like we had just disappeared into thin air. It was amazing, this new world, and the kids were anxious to show it to me.

I was escorted along the wall through a tunnel of branches into the Hall of Flowers. This was a small room big enough to stand up comfortably on a floor littered with pink and white petals. In fact, the theme of pink and white was everywhere, for the outer shell of our room was graced with it in abundance. In between all this vibrant color, little blotches of light filtered through to form round circles on the walls and floor of this grand hall. These circles danced with each wisp of breeze that moved the hall's stately covering giving the space the feel of a fairy ballroom.

We left the Hall of Flowers and made our way in a bent-over fashion down the next tunnel, hugging the brick wall until we came to what they called the Tower of the Sun. This was a semi-open space above the tangle where the kids could climb up and sit on a side branch that peeked out near the top of the wall. This was their lookout to warn the club members of approaching danger. It was known only to them and a stray cat that vanished when it found its hideout invaded.

After the tower came a dark stretch called the Twisted Forest, which was a place of tangled branches so thick that one had to gingerly step over them to reach the next part of the fortress. It was quite the trick in a cotton skirt, yet I was doing a passable job. Now I knew why Noai's skirt was so filthy each night. It was there that I heard Jeremiah's voice call from somewhere outside the hedge, saying, "Momma, someone wants you!" Hans groaned and said under his breath, "Jeremiah, shut up!"

This place was supposed to be kept secret from the entire world, yet Jeremiah, the youngest member of the hideaway band (age fiveish), was about to ruin it. Jeremiah persisted to call since he knew where I was. This put me in quite the dilemma. If I called out of the flower hedge, "What dear?" it would sound rather strange. How could this be explained? It could not. So I said nothing and pretended that I wasn't there, because I wasn't supposed to be. Jeremiah was not easily fooled, as he knew where I was, so he continued to call. There was nothing wrong in his mind about his mom being in the flower bushes, and besides, his reputation was at stake because the African worker,

Amidou, was questioning his report as to where I was. It was frustrating for Jeremiah because every time he called out to me, Amidou would say, "Mama is *not* in the flower bushes!" Yet Jeremiah insisted that I *was* in the flower bushes and kept pointing to them in earnest. It looked like neither one of them was going to give in.

In the meantime, realizing my embarrassing dilemma, I rushed through the Hall of Thorns trying to find my way to the Tower of the Guard to get out before Jeremiah took Amidou's hand and actually led him to the bushes to prove his honesty. What would I do then? In Africa, there are norms of what is and is not acceptable for women to do. Playing in a bougainvillea hedge was definitely not within the norms of polite society for a woman of any age. So, while I was trying to scramble out, Jeremiah was continuing his repartee with Amidou. Surely Amidou would believe him. Amidou in the meantime was repeatedly insisting that "Mama was *not* in the flower bushes and, where *was* she?!"

I finally managed to rather hectically climb over the last tangled limb and emerged from the final exit, sort of intact. I stood up quickly and brushed myself off trying to look as normal as I could, as though I did this every day. I walked forward and approached the stunned Amidou, while his face spread into a slow, wide grin. He commented, "Soooooo, Madame *was* in the flower bushes. You don't say!" At least this cleared Jeremiah's record. He was satisfied; I was not.

I just tossed it off and casually remarked, "Oh, I was just looking at a play spot the kids have. Are you looking for me?" I'm not sure what he thought. African women wouldn't have done something like that. For that matter not a lot of American women would have either. I guess I'm just weird. I guess I always have been. Anyway, I made a mental note on how to coach Jeremiah on the art of evasiveness next time I was in a similar predicament, as I'm sure I would be, many more times in the future.

Pretty soon we had left Bouaké and were back in the village. The children had their whole tropical jungle of a yard again to lose themselves in without being discovered by bothersome African employees. I, too, went back to my daily routine in the home.

CHAPTER SIX

BAKWÉ CULTURE

Culture and language are inseparable and understanding both helps when translating. Before being cleared to translate, Csaba had to write three papers on the study of Bakwé culture from his notes and interviews with people. He ended up writing one paper on Bakwé values, another on the changing Bakwé economic situation, and the last one on sorcery.

The Bakwé value system was interesting. Csaba found that a lack of generosity seemed oddly ranked as a more serious sin than murder or lying. Probably the reasoning behind this was that for people who are trying to eke out a living, sharing food was paramount to survival.

On the economic front, the Bakwé used to be hunters and gatherers. They hunted elephants in the vast underpopulated forest. However, in the last few decades they began selling the forest to immigrants from the north who planted cocoa plantations. With the habitat change, the elephants became scarce.

After a while the land had been sold off and the elephants were gone. The Bakwé then resorted to forms of work that they were not accustomed to. People turned to farming, plantations, clerical positions in the government, teaching, and running small shops and businesses. Unfortunately, other forms of illegitimate work developed too, like prostitution and running rum stills.

The third cultural research paper that Csaba wrote was on sorcery. The Bakwé feared sorcery, and sought ways of protecting themselves, including the use of special charms and fetishes. As Csaba got information and stories, he learned that owls were looked upon as evil. This is because people believed that sorcerers can shape-shift into owls at night, then hold counsels in trees to plan mischief. So, if an owl was heard, the man of the house would go out and yell at the owl, "I can hear you. Get away from my house!"

THE ACCIDENT

A terrible tragedy had happened. The chief was standing off the side of the road with two other men when a small transport bus careened off the road and hit them. Two of the men were killed instantly but the chief remained alive—barely. He was taken to the hospital and died in-route. Everyone was shocked and said that someone in the family was jealous and had used sorcery to cause this horrible accident. Yet in all the speculation, no one had given much thought to the fact that a lot of these vehicles weren't road-worthy or that drivers would pass on a blind curve because they believed their fetishes would protect them.

A Christian friend of ours in the village was disturbed by it. He was beginning to believe what the villagers were saying about the chief that the sorcerers of the village finally got him because he converted. He was the holder of the mask which is the village's mystical connection to the spirit world. When he broke with the old tradition, they said that God couldn't protect him and therefore the sorcerers got him. It was true that the chief had burned all his fetishes (charms) when he had recently become a Christian. But Csaba explained to his troubled friend, "When someone believes like that, then their belief in God is very small. They believe the evil spirits are still ruling the world, but this is not true. The spirits have limited power on earth and no power over God or His people. Since God is sovereign, that accident wasn't caused by someone willing it to happen. It happened because God was in control and allowed it to happen for His reasons. Satan is the father of lies and has bound people up in fear. The Lord reigns supreme and His will and purposes supersede everything else that the devil can do. It is God you should fear. Whenever you are told something contrary to the Bible then you must believe the Bible."

The Christian friend was comforted by these words. It was a new idea that someone was in control even over the spirits and that the Lord reigns supreme. He was very grateful and said to Csaba, "If you hadn't been here to tell me these things, then I would still believe in the ultimate control of the spirits."

The concept of sorcery reflects a different worldview from the one we know in the west. The fear of it is what drives a lot of social interactions and customs. Sorcery is a way to explain the incomprehensible things in life like sickness and death. It also causes an underlying fear and mistrust of your neighbors. It can give rise to an obsession to try to protect yourself from an unseen enemy. It is largely intangible. Originally the Bakwé believed that sorcery, if used by the few, was a way to keep society in line. But recently, they switched to believe that it has turned more into an evil than a good. To understand this concept, you must first understand the Bakwé's view of the world.

According to Csaba's research, the Bakwé don't think sickness and death are natural, and the only time death is thought to be natural is when someone dies of old age. If someone dies sooner than that, they believe something had to have caused it, and someone must be blamed. If someone wanted to do harm to another through sorcery, they could do it through tangible means such as chants and fetish objects which they believed had power, or they could use intangible means such as bad thoughts and dreams. They believed that bad thoughts have conscious, malicious intent which could have power to harm another. Dreams, they believed, were more passive, and a bad dream could mean you were a sorcerer and didn't know it, but you still had subconscious power to harm.

A man recounted to us once that when he was a child he had spoken rashly and said to another child, "I hope you die!" The next day the whole extended family of that boy was there at his doorstep wanting him to recant his curse. They made him renounce publicly what he had said, and then ordered the curse to fall to the ground. Only after that were relations restored. Another man had trouble when he brought home a newer and younger wife to his already disgruntled older one. The two did not get along like he had hoped. In fact, they were downright nasty to each other. When the older wife got pregnant again, the second wife, in a fit of anger said, "You just wait until later!"

Well, as it sometimes happens in this part of the world, the older wife died in childbirth (due to hemorrhaging). Since others remembered what the second wife had said, they blamed her for the killing of the first wife. They said she was jealous and had used her sorcery to harm the other. She was tried and found guilty of murder, then ostracized. She finally had to leave the village due to the animosity that she experienced.

According to this worldview, thoughts have energy and can take form and bring about consequences. The interpersonal conflicts that happen due to this are immense when you are constantly suspecting your neighbor of doing you harm. We asked a Christian man in the village why people used sorcery against others, and he felt it was all due to jealousy. People see others with things they want and are jealous of them. They then seek to harm the person who has those things. Instead of helping each other advance, they get jealous and tear one another down to keep everyone at the same low level. A common belief in West Africa is that there is only so much good in the world to go around, so if you have more, then another will automatically have less. That means you must bring others down to your level. It is difficult for a society to get ahead this way. The longer we were in the village, the more we realized that Satan works his greatest tricks through deception. It was a joy to see Christians breaking out of that fear by turning to God, who is all-powerful.

As missionaries, we had a lot to learn. We could only see so much and needed to trust God that He would cause His light to reach into their darkness and open up their prison. We also couldn't fathom the depths of that darkness. Yet, on the other hand, if we could really see all the wonderful riches of God's grace and power in all its fullness, we wouldn't be able to fathom that as well either. It would go beyond our wildest imaginings. We just needed to know that God's light would swallow up all darkness in victory, the victory paid for by the blood of His Son.

CHAPTER SEVEN

DECEPTION

Not everything is true that meets the eye. Some things are cleverly hidden from view that would change everyone's opinion. So why do we believe what we see at first glance?

Alexis saw something on Ivorian TV and told Csaba about it. There was a French man who got up and said, "What you are about to see is being filmed live." The camera zoomed in on an African man announcing to a crowd, "I will cure your diseases, I will cure infertility, I will chase away sorcerers, and tell you your future. Come and watch."

Then this diviner pointed to a spectator in the crowd and accused him of being a sorcerer. Stunned, the man got up and started to shake all over, then fell down dead. The diviner announced with authority, "Since he was a sorcerer, by my power he had a heart attack and he's now dead." Then the diviner said some incantations and raised him miraculously from the dead with his great power. The crowd was incredulous as the man got up dazed and walked away.

Next a crazy person walked into the crowd and the diviner went over to him and said something to him. The man crumpled to the floor. The crowd was astonished. After a few more things were whispered to him, the crazy man got up and was instantly in his right mind. There were murmurs of approval from the crowd. The diviner stopped what he was doing and announced to everyone that for a price, he would use his power to help whoever needed it. People from all over started to crowd in to get his services. The cameraman interviewed the crowd about what they thought of this diviner. One man responded, "I've never seen anything like this before. Since I've seen this now with my own eyes, I'm convinced." Other people exclaimed likewise that this was so.

Then the French man got up and announced, "Ladies and Gentlemen, this was a hoax. We are a paid troupe of actors. The crazy man and the man who supposedly died were both actors. We wanted to show you that you were capable of being cleverly deceived. We want you to know that there are a lot of people out there who are trying to do the same thing to deceive you for your money. Beware!"

Then the TV interviewed the crowd again, but the response was different from what one would have expected. One man said, "I don't care what that French man has said. I saw it with my own eyes and believe in this power. I want it!"

I was amazed. How could people be so easily deceived? Csaba reminded me that their worldview was different. If they had been told from infancy to believe in these things, then they are more likely to be deceived. One day, a similar event occurred in Touadji II.

THE YACOUBA WOMAN

There was a powerful Yacouba woman, a diviner, who was believed to have mystical powers. People believed that these powers could chase away the sorcerers who were the cause of the evil in their villages. Since Touadji II had a lot of sick people dying at that time, they felt it must be due to sorcery, so they sought this woman out. They were interested in her because other villages had reported that she had successfully chased away sorcerers from their villages too.

We heard how this woman operated. She went around the village and prophetically revealed who she thought was a sorcerer. If these people didn't confess to the truth, she put them through a trial by ordeal to prove her case. The trial given to the suspect was to hold out an iron kettle at arm's length for a long time. If the kettle got heavy and the accused person's arms dipped, then he or she was guilty. Once a person's guilt was proved, he or she had to pay a large sum of money to the diviner and then be ostracized by the village. Csaba's colleagues (Alexis, Perez, and Firmain) were shaking their heads over this until they found out that she was coming to our village. This alarmed the guys so much that they got together and prayed that God would expose this woman for what she was, a deceiver.

She arrived one evening with her team. They were escorted to a house where she and some of the elders of Touadji II discussed the problems of the village way into the wee hours of the morning. After they were done, the woman slipped into the dark to do her work. She stalked around the sleeping village house by house, courtyard by courtyard, clinking softly on a can. As she tapped it, she supposedly gained knowledge as to who was a real sorcerer.

The next morning, she set to work. She walked around the village with her men trying to mystically locate all the sorcerers that her can had revealed to her in the night. She stopped at the courtyard of a widow, whose husband died not too long ago. While a crowd gathered around her, the diviner accused the poor woman of having killed her husband through sorcery, and also of burning her neighbor's house down as well. Everyone knew this house. It had been the talk of the village for months. This was the very house that had burned when her neighbor's second wife knocked over a lantern, which caused the house to go up in flames. Of course, everyone knew that sorcery was involved or why would it have happened in the first place? Now the villagers knew who was responsible and who to blame.

These accusations did not go over well with the widow or her grown children. They were being accused of mishaps that were not their doing. They were also in danger of being ostracized by the very people they relied upon. Her eldest son was so enraged that he stripped down to his shorts and got ready to fight. Unbelievably, her grown daughters did the same to show their extreme indignation. So, with this mass of fuming flesh in shorts moving towards her, the Yacouba woman decided to quickly take her leave. She was not wanted, and she knew it.

When Csaba and his guys heard what had happened, they all shook their heads. There was not much they could do, until Perez's mother, also a widow, was accused. The Bakwé translation team had been working at the office when someone came in and said, "Perez, they've got your mother!" Perez shot out of his chair and stormed off to his courtyard where he saw his mother holding an iron kettle out in front of her, sweating hard. She was old and the kettle was very heavy, but she had to hold out longer and prove her innocence or the village would ostracize her. Then she'd have to pay a penalty she could ill afford.

At the sight of his aged mother standing there so pitifully, Perez stormed into the courtyard and grabbed the kettle out of his mother's hands. He shoved her in the house and shut the door behind her, giving a parting order to stay inside. The crowd got angry at this intrusion. They wanted the death of her husband explained so the trial would have to be continued. The Yacouba woman also wanted to get on with her work so she could be paid. They all ordered Perez to get his mother out. Perez refused and was ready to fight anyone who resisted his decision.

Faced with a six-foot steaming Perez, the group left, but swore that they would be back the next day to force her to take the trial. Perez came back to the office and the group decided what could be done. Csaba went into town and consulted a lawyer to find out what they could do legally. The law said that if this Yacouba woman forced people to do the trial or if she disturbed the peace, then the law could step in. Csaba had the guys write a letter of complaint to the mayor. Then the next day, the mayor had an official go to the village and tell them that they couldn't touch Perez's mother. She was now safe, but the rest of the village was not. The Bakwé translation team had prayed that God would expose this diviner woman for what she was, and they had only to wait on God to answer their prayer.

Back in the village, the Yacouba woman and her men went on to another house that harbored suspected sorcerers. She stood before the little house and said in her prophetic way, "There is a woman here who has a recently deceased husband who . . . " She went through a long string of prophetic utterances that accused the woman. The only problem was that she got her information wrong. The husband had long been deceased and everyone knew it. A murmur of disapproval went up through the crowd. The accused gained confidence by this mix-up and refused the trial.

Then the woman left and went to another courtyard with a long list of accusations, but mixed up on one vital point there too. The accused was not paralyzed like she had said, and this person was brought out walking for all to see. More doubt went around the group and the trial was not carried out there either. The Yacouba woman was getting nervous as she felt the tide turn against her. She needed some success fast, so she moved on to another courtyard hoping to redeem herself. But this was not to be either, for she messed up that time too. The final clincher came when she had her helpers unearth a supposed mystical pot that she said was at the root of all their problems and it would be hidden somewhere in the village. This was her last trump card. If the villagers could see her destroy an evil thing that had caused them so much trouble, then they would finally believe her, and she could get paid.

One of her helpers ran around the village trying to find the mystical pot. He eventually stopped behind a house then supposedly dug it up when no one was looking. As it was brought out triumphantly for all to see, someone in the crowd said, "Hey, that looks like the same pot that I saw unearthed in another village by this woman."

Someone else added, "If it was just dug up, why is there no dirt on it?"

Another person responded, "It's because she washed it."

"Then why is it not wet?"

Doubt was going through the crowd about their wonder-woman and her mysterious pot. Finally, after much disillusionment and with so many of the accused refusing to admit that they were sorcerers, the woman couldn't continue on. She said that she was being blocked by something. In parting, she went over to complete a final act by burying another special protection pot behind the house of the old man of the village that would kill any remaining sorcerers and bring peace and health to the village.

The woman left, but did peace and health come to the village? Shortly after this, the old man of the village became sick. Health had not come to him. Later he died. Was the village happy now? The only thing that they had accomplished by bringing this woman into the village was more infighting erupting between families who now had new grudges against each other due to the accusations. She had deceived them all, and they had believed her until God answered a few men's prayers that turned this woman's evil work upside down. Through this happening, the villagers could at least begin to see that health, peace, and prosperity hadn't come by these means.

CHAPTER EIGHT

THE WILDS BEYOND

Since living in a village could be intense with all that
was going on, we enjoyed getting out in the jungle part
of our backyard as an escape. Our family loved camping
and we certainly had the yard to do it in. It was a treat
to camp, but not everyone saw things the way we did.

CAMPING FOR THE MENTALLY UNBALANCED

It was dry season, and we decided to put up tents in the back section of our property for when our missionary friends came with their four kids. The section that we wanted to camp in was behind the ponds in a grassy area under a tree surrounded by a hedge of flowers. No one went back there except our workers on occasion. It was a camper's dream.

The boys were going to sleep out the first night, and the rest of us would take a turn later when we were more set up with the full regalia of mattresses and pillows. When Alexis and his wife came to see us, Csaba mentioned that we had set up the tents in the back and that the boys and their friends were going to sleep out in them that night. Alexis shook his head and said, "You put your guests out back in the bush?! I know they are only kids, but still, we would never do *that* to a guest, even if it was only a child. It would be an insult."

Csaba explained that in the States, each year, even the wealthy will don old clothes to replace their fine ones, leave their nice homes, and drive far out on rough roads into the wilderness with their cars. They will then hike for hours over perilous paths to pick the most secluded spot to pitch their makeshift dwelling on hard ground. After that, they will spend hours catching their dinner in the stream. Then if they are lucky to have actually caught anything, they will clean their fish and then cook them over an open fire, and supplement it with little packets of dried food. They will do this for their whole vacation, until it is time they are forced back to the city to their nice homes at the holiday's end.

Alexis just shook his head and said, "Why would anyone want to leave a perfectly good house that you have spent lots of money on and go live in a tent? Why would anyone want to cook their food over an open fire when you have the luxury of a stove in your own home? If we did that, people at best would think we were unbalanced and at worst they would think we were stark raving mad. How barbaric!"

Csaba hadn't mentioned that the second night our honored guests, the adults, were going to sleep out there too. It was best that we just didn't mention these things. Yet, it's all a matter of perspective. According to us, the choice place is in the tent. I had even dragged mattresses out there with pillows and everything. It was going to be great. We had plastic chairs set up around the campfire. We had planned to cook hot dogs and eat cookies with hot chocolate which were all a luxury in Africa. Were we unbalanced? Some people would have thought so. I guess it was just a matter of perspective.

To the folks in the village, a mark of prosperity was to own fine clothes and a fine house. If they had the means, they sought to get away from their open fires and drafty mud-and-stick houses. If they had arrived at that level of prosperity, they would not think of going back to living like they had before, because where was the sense in it all?

Yet we enjoyed camping because we were in nature, seeing the grandeur of the night sky, hearing the wind playing in the trees, and being kept awake by those irritating frogs that called to their mates all night. We loved it all. Our backyard had proven to be a big blessing indeed, a veritable camper's paradise. Our camping spot was pretty wild, but there were even wilder portions in our yard still.

SECRET FORTS

Camping only happened during the height of dry season, but the rest of the year there were other things to do out of doors that were not brought to a halt by a thunderstorm.

My kids always had this compelling urge to explore, and I often saw them sneaking away with their machetes to go into the tangled jungle of our backyard. Once in the wildest sections, they would chop out hidden passages that would end in secret hideaways. From this, the game of "secret forts" took shape. What was a secret fort? It was a hidden place deep in the bush that only you knew about, where you could steal away undetected and remain in oblivion for hours until someone found you. If you were found out, the finder would yell in triumph, "Ah ha!" This meant you would have to make another secret fort because the main appeal of doing it in the first place was to keep your fort hidden from the world. The other goal was to find and expose everyone else's secret fort. It was like a grand treasure hunt in the forest.

In his firsthand account, Hans writes,

> I took a machete and snuck out to the back of our property. Since carrying a machete always aroused suspicion in my younger siblings, I had to hide it in my shirt. After making sure I was not followed, I scoured the back passages and paths for any promising piece of bush that might let me chop through it to somewhere hidden without leaving a trace of the entrance. I spied a tall group of banana trees clumped in the bush to the left of our property. It was encircled by a mass of tangled, thick vines and branches. I thought this clump of banana trees would make a great fort, so I tunneled into the ten-foot mass below and chopped out an entrance that led inside its enclosure. The tunnel was low enough to crawl through, yet it still remained hidden since I piled dead leaves and brush at the entrance to conceal it.
>
> As I pushed through the greenery and started to chop, I kept low to the ground trying to remain hidden. After chopping several yards from the entrance, I had no more need for a tunnel, so I stood up and cut a clear path to the banana trees. Two fears were now in my mind. The first was

that the sound of my chopping would soon lead an inquisitive brother or sister to my fort. I really did not want to see an eager face peering in at my entrance saying, "Ah ha!" This would only ruin everything secret about my fort, and I'd have to start all over again.

The second and more prominent of my fears was that I would come face to face with a snake. Fortunately, neither of these fears were realized, and I made a small clearing in the banana trees without incident. After I finished clearing it out, I sat down and enjoyed the secrecy and silence of my new fort. I enjoyed staring up at the smooth, green trunks of the banana trees with their papery giant leaves that rustled in the wind. If I was lucky enough, I would keep this fort secret for a long time.

I have entered several of my children's forts, and some were difficult indeed. As I crawled on my hands and knees into the impenetrable mass of tangle, I thought about snakes and wondered what fool mom would let her kids do this? Anyhow, the one fort that I didn't end up in was the one that existed at the top of an old oil palm. Oil palms have ragged spikes going all the way up the trunk and can be quite painful if you hit them the wrong way. Hans and Jeremiah teamed up together, climbed up the palm, and wedged a board

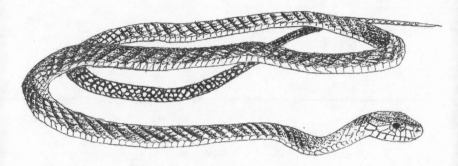

for a sitting area in the crown. I didn't know about this fort until the snake incident occurred.

One day Hans was climbing his palm tree quietly to avoid arousing the keen ears of Andreas and Noai, when he met a green mamba in his fort. The snake was not supposed to be there, but since it was, Hans decided that he would just climb right down and leave the fort to the snake, as he wished for no further encounters with this deadly visitor.

The secret forts continued on for a long time and after we went on furlough our property reverted to its natural, kid-less state. Then I went back to thinking of other things besides what dangers my kids were tunneling into and what they would meet slithering at the other end.

CHAPTER NINE

THE TRANSLATION PROCESS

Csaba was finally cleared to start translation. He officially chose Alexis to be his co-translator, and Alexis would end up being invaluable to Csaba as they worked together in the years to come.

Translation wasn't an easy task. To translate a passage, Csaba first studied the Greek text of the New Testament, identifying any potential textual problems. Then he read and compared the different commentaries to understand the meaning of the text. As he did this, he made notes in French and jotted down suggestions for how the translation should go. He then drafted the verse in Bakwé and passed it on to Alexis. Alexis read these notes and compared the French translations and commentary he had on the passages. He then took Csaba's translation and made changes. If he found too many problems with Csaba's translation, he then drafted the verse over again himself. After this, he passed it back to Csaba. Csaba then compared it back with the Greek and his exegetical notes. He made notes of questions he had and marked down further suggestions which went back to Alexis. This process was possible because Csaba had become so familiar with the language over the years.

Going back and forth like this they came up with the best translation of the passage. They did this, verse by verse, chapter by chapter of the entire book that they were currently working on. When they were finished with the book, they would pass it over to Perez and Firmain who took the manuscript and read it out loud to different audiences in the village. After getting this wider feedback, they jotted down notes where people had difficulty following or had made suggestions. Csaba and Alexis then looked at these notes to see if any changes were warranted.

An example of a change that could be made based on these notes is the use of a full noun in the place of a pronoun. In other words, where the text used a *he, she,* or *it* needed to be made more explicit by using a full noun, so the reader was not confused as to who was speaking. Other times they needed to find a better word for a concept that was new to the hearer, or they needed to put in a footnote to explain a biblical custom that was confusing.

When they were happy with their changes, they passed the translation back to Perez or Firmain to do a back translation, which was translating the book from Bakwé back into a literal French. This back translation would then be sent to a Wycliffe translation consultant in preparation for a verse by verse check of the translation. This check and any final changes would have to be made before the book could be published. It was a long painstaking process, but all these checks make for a good translation.

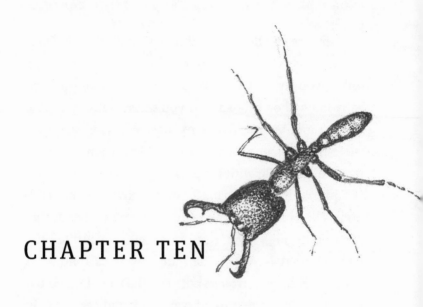

CHAPTER TEN

BRAVE DEEDS

While the translators were doing their thing, we, back
on the home front, busied ourselves with more unusual
and interesting pursuits, or at least my kids did. Kids
are kids no matter where they live and they like to
have fun. Mine were no exception. One of the more
unique games they created had to do with the Spartan
forces of the insect world—driver ants.

These ants will swarm across a path in a rampage and
attack anything in their way. If you happen to put your
foot down in the middle of the army, they will take this
to be a declaration of war and crawl up your leg to do
battle. The pinchers of the guard ants are so long that
they can even be used as sutures. The pinchers of the

workers are smaller and feel like a smaller prick. Once the army gets a hold of your skin, they will not let go unless you forcibly remove them. A driver ant is basically latched on till death. If you see someone jumping around and yelling like a maniac, you can safely assume he has met with an army of driver ants who are now doing battle with his legs.

You may be wondering how this involved my children. They had somehow gotten it into their heads that running through a river of driver ants constituted fun and signified bravery. The game went as follows: A child would find a troop of drivers that had fanned out in a raid where the ground was black and crawling. In this mass of swarming ants, there were usually little pockets of ant-less islands. These islands were crucial to the game because a child would try to judge what island he must hop to in order to reach the other side, which was hopefully devoid of ants.

If there were no more islands to be had and the child needed to make a dash for it through the river of ants, all he had to do was stamp his feet fast enough while running for all he was worth to reach the other end unscathed. If the particular child hesitated at any point in his journey, or didn't stamp hard enough, then the driver ants would start their ascent up his leg. This would cause the child, once he reached the other end, to hop around like a maniac until all the ants had been routinely removed. So, during the season of the driver ant invasions, I could sometimes look out my window and see children dashing and laughing or hopping and yelling depending on the success of their attempts. It was definitely an alternative way to spend an afternoon.

Driver ants were not the only things that held fascination. The next brave deed was to arouse the wrath of the "killer mom-hen." We had one hen in particular that must have had an overdose of mothering hormones because once her chicks hatched, she became savage. One could even surmise that she had rabies, if that were possible. The kids didn't realize this until one day, as Jeremiah walked out the back door, something hit him hard from behind and low to the ground. Jeremiah wheeled around to be confronted by an irate hen that threw all her three pounds worth straight at his leg. He had evidently committed the unforgivable sin of entering her personal space that housed her darling offspring. Jeremiah just pushed her away, but she came back with a vengeance.

Once the children realized this little quirk of hers, they challenged the hen to battle by fanning their hands out in front of her face. Once her hackles were up, she would

rush in for the attack by leaping high and thrashing her spindly chicken legs to scratch her enemy. If the kids were quick enough, they would remove their hands before she actually clawed them. But alas, the hen was a good fighter, and this meant scratches for the human combatants.

Hans fought her the most successfully by taking off his rubber sandal, holding it before her face with a challenge she couldn't refuse. It was comical to watch our mother hen fighting a sandal for all she was worth with her wee children peeping their encouragement in the background. Even when the sandal was dropped, our mother hen continued to attack it on the ground to make sure that it was, indeed, dead. This didn't say much about her intelligence.

The last brave deed that the children attempted was instigated by their father. He hadn't planned this one; it just happened. You see, Csaba raised local African killer bees. Why are they called killer bees? Who knows, but maybe it was due to their highly excitable nature, and the fact that they were more aggressive in defending their hive than other bees. For these reasons, Csaba had to work them at night. And on one of these nights, the kids wanted to go with him. Since there was only one other bee suit, it was given to Noai. The rest were to watch from a distance in the shadows, since these bees at night will only attack a moving object around a light. Csaba was delighted to show the kids his hobby and got Noai ready. I was a bit skeptical, since I didn't trust bees as a general rule. I just liked their honey.

The crew set out for the hive, with the two bee-suited ·individuals and their lanterns out front, while the three unprotected children with no light were at a distance behind. Everything went well until the cloud of highly irate bees found an opening in Noai's hood. The suit was too big for her and a tiny gap no bigger than a finger, presented itself right in the neckline. Pretty soon her hood was filling up with bees that were crawling all over her face. She called out softly, "Daddy."

Csaba, busy with the hive, mumbled back, "What dear?"

Noai nervously responded, "Daddy, look!"

Csaba turned around and found Noai's face crawling with bees on the inside of her hood. He was a bit startled and told her to remain calm. Thankfully she did so. If she had panicked, it would have been bad since the bees will sting if provoked by fast movement but might not if she kept her movements relaxed. He walked her slowly out of the lantern light, gently took off her hood then softly brushed away the bees one by one. Fortunately, she only got stung three times. But on the way back to the house, the boys in the shadows were too interested in what was going on and they got too close. Jeremiah then got stung because the bees were following the movement up to the house in the fringe of the lantern light. After everyone came into the house, I treated Noai and Jeremiah's stings. Then Hans decided to take her place. He went out with Csaba but came back within five minutes. He too got stung because of a gap in his cloth. Csaba just had to work those bees alone. After caring for the stings, the bees were forgiven since we all got a large jar full of rich African honey.

Killer bees aside, I never quite knew what my kids would be up to next and it wouldn't have surprised me if I were to come upon a leopard trap on one of my walks in the wild section of our property. But instead of a leopard trap, one day before a storm hit, I came upon what looked like three overgrown monkeys clinging onto the tall stalks in our bamboo patch. On second look I found these were not overgrown monkeys, but my three sons up in the bamboo swaying with the wind. I looked farther and saw another dark shape bobbing beyond them which turned out to be my daughter. She too was clinging on a stalk and looking quite wild. When the wind picked up with the incoming storm, the bamboo swayed in opposing directions with the blast. Since the kids' feet were on different stalks, it looked like they were riding unruly horses that they were constantly trying to gather in. I guess the idea was to not get thrown off your horse, because if you did, you would get spiked on the way down by the hard-pointed knobs of the bamboo. That actually happened to Noai during one of her bamboo rides and she needed to be taken to the city for stitches. But what is excitement without a little danger? One thing for sure was that life in the village was never boring.

CHAPTER ELEVEN

NORMAL DAYS

Other days were not so drastically exciting. They were just normal days with all the beauty and fun a day could bring in the tropics.

I walked down to our pond and stood there silently watching. It was morning and the pond was alive with activity. Dragonflies with blue tails zipped above the water like little stealth helicopters. Occasionally one would dip down and hit the top of the water with its tail, then dart back up to join the others hovering in the

air. Metallic blue butterflies danced dreamily amongst the trees as if
they had no care in
the world.

A   cry
pierced
the air and
a brilliant king-
fisher   in   neon
colors   swooped
down to the pond's surface, slic-
ing the water with its orange beak
before dashing up to its perch in a tree. Then out of a
thick tangle of lush growth popped a shy, black bird
with long, orange legs. He waddled slowly, poking methodically at the mud until I made a movement when
he quietly vanished. A few frogs took flying leaps dis-
appearing into the water, only to resurface later with
their telescope eyes warily watching me.

By now the sun was peeping over the tops of the
trees and the pond reflected the greenery around it like
a giant painting in a haze of humidity. Racing on this
watery canvas were black bugs brushing strokes that
disappeared almost as soon as they were painted on.

So much activity in the morning, so much life! But
it would all die down again to a lethargic pace as the
heat intensified and my kids came down to play.

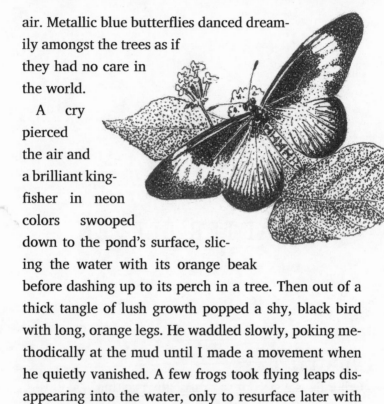

❅⊕❅

When school stopped for the summer, Andreas wanted to take up boating on the high seas of our murky
pond for his leisure activity. His only problem was that
he had no boat. This was quickly solved by felling some
bamboo, letting them dry a little in the sun, then ty-
ing them together with cords. When he launched it in
the water, the bamboo raft proved less than desirable
because it rode about three inches under the water. I
guess he hadn't let the bamboo dry long enough. But
the effects of his boat looked comical because I could
only see a boy partially submerged in water up to his
waist, slowly gliding around the pond.

This was not satisfactory, so Andreas brought his ship
on shore and strung a row of empty plastic jugs underneath with a rubber cord. This gave the boat an acceptable amount of buoyancy. He then made an oar out of
an old piece of wood so that he could sail his seas kay-
ak-style. The boat worked fairly well, even though the
back part still rode somewhat under the water. But all
mechanical problems aside, he found that he could go
pretty fast if he remained in the center of the boat. If
he failed to remember this little quirk of boat balance,
his craft would tip to one side causing the empty jugs
to break loose and fly out, thus dumping their proud
captain into the pea green seas to fend for himself. Yet
despite its quirks, all in all it was enough of a success
to make for an enjoyable ride. Between the raft and his
old bodysurfing board, boating would continue until

all would be disturbed by an abominable sea monster named Luther.

We had recently bought a German Shepherd pup which we named Luther. He was meant to be a guard dog, and we trained him initially on kitty treats. He responded well on the treats but so did the cats. When I asked the dog to sit, the dog would sit, and so did the cats. When I asked the dog to come, the dog came and so did the cats. Luther became well trained as a guard dog and so did the cats until we ran out of kitty treats and the cats went back to their aloof, feline existence.

Luther was extremely possessive of our family, guarding us from everything—good and bad alike. As he grew, Luther turned into the most splendid, black, longhaired Shepherd I have ever seen. He had a power-ful broad chest, long straight ears and bright chestnut markings in the shape of a crescent on the side of his beautifully shaped head. But as he grew, we noticed that he had an obsession for saving things. We first dis-covered this quirk when I took him down to the pond one day while the kids were swimming.

Andreas was enjoying the pond while he paddled around on his bodysurfing board. When the dog saw Andreas, he became agitated. He whined in his wor-ried way, pulled at his leash, and strained to go into the pond. Not sure of what he wanted, I let him off leash. Once unrestrained, Luther raced quickly to the bank of the pond, took one flying leap down the six-foot bank and landed splash into the water. He then swam with powerful strokes to where Andreas was floating, grabbed the string of the board in his mouth and pulled Andreas back to shore. He wasn't content with just that, but kept pulling the board, minus Andreas, up the steep bank. When he reached the top, he deposited his burden, shook the water off his fur, then looked to me for congratulations on saving my child.

The capsized and flustered Andreas came up the bank to retrieve his board and then returned in a huff to the pond to continue floating. He wasn't going to stop his fun due to this misguided dog. Luther, on seeing the child in distress again, jumped off the bank once more, and swam out to rescue his victim. This time Andreas started paddling furiously in the opposite direction to get away from his unwanted lifeguard, splashing him in the face as best he could. The dog was adamant, though, and made a beeline straight for Andreas. Luther grabbed the rope once again and pulled Andreas back to safety where he was supposed to stay. At this point, Andreas decided to give up on his surfboard and brought out the old bamboo raft instead. It was so heavy a body could hardly lift it, let alone the fool dog. Maybe he would be left alone this time. But no luck, since Luther did the same life-dog-thing except with a lot more difficulty. Attempting to tote a large bamboo raft with a bunch of detergent jugs underneath up a bank was definitely a challenge but not too much for a determined guard dog. In fact, no matter what the kids were paddling on, the dog would save them from it. This certainly put a damper on water activities.

Finally, we realized that if the kids wanted to have any fun at all in the pond, they would just have to tie up their self-appointed lifeguard to a tree and leave him whimpering in the shade.

CHAPTER TWELVE

CHALLENGES

Each book of the Bible that was translated had its own level of difficulty and challenges. Csaba found that the books of Romans and Hebrews were the hardest to translate in the New Testament. Romans was difficult because of the heavy information load. Condensed information in each sentence in the Greek often had to be translated by several words in Bakwé. The sentences ended up being really long since there was not a one-to-one correlation in words between the two languages. What complicated it further was that sentences in Paul's epistles were already long to begin with. This meant that they had to break up some longer sentences to keep the reader from confusion. Hebrews was difficult to translate because of its higher literary style and how it used numerous Greek literary devices in the author's argumentation. It also included many quotes from the Old Testament that move in and out of the text to support the arguments.

The gospel of Mark and the book of Philemon were the easiest. Csaba was advised to start with the gospel of Mark, not only because it was a short gospel, but because it had the easiest Greek of all the gospels. And, it was strategic to get a gospel translated into a booklet so the church could start using it. Surprisingly, Revelation was not as difficult as one would think because it had a lot of imagery which was not the job of the translator to interpret, but only to translate. The word *revelation* in Bakwé was translated as *To-the-eyes-come-things*.

Outside of the Bible translation challenges, we as a family had to deal with our own challenges of living in a village as well. We lived in a place that was not only exciting and wonderful, but also demanding and at times very hard. Living in a village was like taking a drink from a fire hose. While water is a good thing, if it comes in high enough doses, it can smack you in the face and knock you off your feet.

What was challenging about living in a village? We were constantly on display, being watched and followed wherever we went because we could never blend into any crowd. We could not predict when we'd be needed to solve another crisis that popped up, which put us on demand at any hour, even at night. This was called living in your work. And the downside of living with so many people in close quarters was that inevitably we just needed a break from it all.

God gave us that break out in the back of our property which consisted of several acres of fruit trees, gardens, flowers, two ponds, and the wild section beyond bordered by a teak forest that I had planted. On this property we could go back and escape from the many demands of village life and recharge, unwatched by the world. It was peaceful there, something the village was often not.

We didn't want to take ourselves out of the village since it was our ministry. Yet if we stayed there too long, we would inevitably get run down and have to leave. This was why our back property meant so much to us. It was an island of comfort in a sea of difficulty. Unfortunately, that island was being threatened.

THE BULLDOZER

At the beginning of our stay in the village, we were given land and told that someday the village was going to be broken up into city blocks with roads so that electricity could be put in. Our border by the road could change by about ten feet, they said, and that was OK by us. We planted up the property and left a fifteen-foot buffer on the roadside. When we came back from our first furlough, we were told that a committee had drawn up official plans to break the village into lots. They then called up a surveyor to put in the markers which made it official. Once it was official, it could not be changed.

The results were interesting. They planned that the prized football field would move from where it was on the other side of the village to be placed on our back land, which had drainage problems along with a sloping, irregular terrain that ended in marshland. After cutting our land off in the back, they gave us some scrubland across the road that belonged to another higher-up in the village named Foley. Foley was very upset by it all and still claimed his land.

We were caught in the middle since we couldn't develop the new land without offending Mr. Foley and our existing land with its fruit trees would be cut in half and put into a football field that would be useless on marshy ground. The proposed road through our property that bordered the football field would lead to nowhere except the marsh and there were no houses beyond that.

It sickened me to see a road go through the special places that we had always used as a family, a road that seemed to have no purpose. It would take out the mango tree plus the hammocks, cross through the cocoa forest, and take out the oranges, sour sop, guava, and a grapefruit tree. It would ruin the rice field and the grassy corner where we had always put up our tents, and would allow open access to the back of our property, the wild section, which meant that there would be nowhere else to escape to anymore.

Yet, could I trust God that He knew best and that if He took this area away from us, that He would give another one in its place? Csaba tried to talk to the chief and asked him if something couldn't be changed. He was told in an indirect way that once a map is official and markers put in, it was like the law of the Medes and Persians—irrevocable. Evidently others had been upset and wanted their boundaries changed too. To all of them, there was but one answer—no. I had a rough time giving this one up to the Lord. I kept yielding it only to take it back again to fret once more. Finally, I realized that God had given me this land as one of His many blessings and now I must be willing to give it back if He chose to take it away. I needed to look to Him for how He would meet my future needs in living in this difficult environment.

The village wasn't ready to bulldoze yet, since they needed the capital first. That would be hard to get from people who had already given in the past only to have their money go down a black hole of corruption twice now. So we enjoyed what we had in the meantime, savoring it to the fullest knowing we were on borrowed time, a time that was now a gift and no longer a right. We had picnics back by our favorite climbing tree, ate the fruit of our orange trees that finally started bearing, and often went out to sit on the grass to be alone with God in such beauty and peace. So in the coming years, I prayed that God would spare our land, even though I couldn't see a way around it.

When we came back after our second furlough, there was talk again of it going through, but this time more seriously. Since no one really thought they would actually do it that year, we put in a large rice field of three acres at the outer fringes of our property. Our neighbors put in their rice field too on our side border like they had always done in years past. Life went on as normal. Our rice was almost ready to harvest when we got word that the village finally collected enough money and was looking for a bulldozer. They had to do it soon since the government was ready to match funds, and the electricity was coming to the nearby market town. If our village didn't do it now, they would miss their chance.

There was a flurry of activity as people dismantled their houses and moved to new lots. It was a bitter-sweet thing in everyone's mind. The village had wanted electricity for a long time, and this was a way to get it even if it meant destroyed rice fields, broken houses and disgruntled neighbors in the process.

The bulldozer arrived and started on the main roads that were on the far side of the village. As the day wore on, more and more roads were put in. Our neighbor's rice field was taken out when a road went through the field between us. Our field was still intact because the back road through our property hadn't been done yet. The second day of work, the bulldozer broke down. The man needed a gift of money to get it going again; Csaba gave it to him to show the village that he cared about their needs and was behind their progress. But we were still praying that somehow our back road wouldn't be done.

The third day, we noticed that the noise from the bulldozer had stopped again. Csaba went to check and found that the bulldozer had broken down a second time. Someone was sent to get a part in San Pedro, which wasted time. During this delay, the driver got a message from his boss that he was needed on a job somewhere else. He would need to finish what he could by the end of the day, then leave the next morning. This wouldn't be too hard since most of the village was already done. The electricity could come now. There just remained a few fringe roads of no significance which included our own back road. When the part finally came at noon, he started up his machine and went to finish off the last bit. We realized that there would not be time to do all the roads. I had hoped and prayed fervently that ours would not be one of them.

In the meantime, Csaba helped out wherever he could by finding stakes and guiding the bulldozer. He wanted to make sure the village knew that he was behind their efforts to get electricity. He noticed the time slipping away. Just then, with an hour to go till quitting time, the command was given, and the bulldozer turned toward our road. It started to come our way. Csaba held his breath as he judged the distance to our property and the time left.

At the same moment, Janvier left our house and went to check on the progress of the bulldozer as well.

He had been praying for days that the bulldozer would not come our way and that the rice and our back property could be saved. As he looked in the direction of the noise, he saw the bulldozer veering towards us. He put in a last urgent plea for God to act. As he did so, the bulldozer suddenly changed direction and went off to another part of the village. Janvier thanked God and went back inside. As far as he was concerned the matter was settled.

Csaba told me later what had happened. There was a rich man who supposedly paid off the director of affairs to not put in the allotted road by his house so that he could put a shop there instead. Other people got wind of it and were mad because their rice fields and homes had been destroyed even after they put in a plea for change as well, just like us. Because this man was rich, they suspected that he had paid off the driver, so they were upset and complained to the chief.

The chief was told that this man had made a deal to reroute the bulldozer until there was no more time left for his road. Since only thirty minutes remained and an argument was brewing, the chief ordered the bulldozer to stop in its tracks and put in this other disputed road instead. That's the point where Janvier had been praying and saw it turn. After the other road was put in, it was quitting time. Since the driver had another job to do the next day, he loaded the machine onto his truck and was gone. Our property and our rice were saved by default. It would be ours until the village got enough money to do this last unused fringe road which at the time of this writing many years later, still remains undone. It was a small request to our God in the grand scheme of things, but He had mercy on us, and gave that land back as a gift.

CHAPTER THIRTEEN

ACQUIRING KEY TERMS

Settling on key biblical terms such as *love, mercy, hope, justice, righteousness, grace,* etc., was crucial and took some time because Csaba involved the Bakwé from the churches in different villages. This was necessary because they were already starting to use their own terms when they did oral translations of a passage on Sundays. Csaba found that often the translation of these terms was not the best, and we didn't want them to be perpetuated in the Christian community.

For example, people were translating *angel* and *prophet* with the same term. The term *Holy Spirit* was being translated in a number of different ways and we needed to find just one. So at the meetings, Csaba would explain the term from the Greek and why certain words would not work. Then he asked for their opinion on what word would best fit that concept. He would discuss with them the pros and cons of each term. These discussions were very helpful, and they were well received.

If no good word could be found, a solution was to transliterate a term from the Greek. The word *angel* had to be transliterated into Bakwé, like it has been done in most languages of the world. For terms like *spirit, soul, body,* or *flesh,* they found good words. The word for *repentance,* however, was harder to find, as well as the term *to forgive.*

REPENTANCE

Often when translating from one language to another the translator may not find a one-word equivalent for a single Greek word. When this happened, they needed to use a string of words to get the meaning across. This was the case for the word *repentance,* which in Bakwé is *toro 'lı balʋ -wälı.* This meant literally in English *to abandon sin.* The assumption is that you are carrying sin around with you as a way of life. When you repent of your sins, you abandon them and turn to God. It was as close as the team could get to the Greek idea of turning from sin and turning to God in a complete changing of one's attitude towards God.

Other key words that needed to use a phrase instead of just one word were these:

prophet: "God in-the-mouth-speak-person" (*nyɔsʋamlıpalanyɔɔ*)

the promises of God: "the thing that God said that he would do/give" (*wiili Nyɔsʋa 'daaa' 'ɔmä -nyı*)

prophesy: "to speak-God's-mouth" or "to speak for God" (*palanyɔsʋamlı*)

After coming back from these trips to the outlying villages Csaba was satisfied that he was closer to getting the right terms. The meetings also helped because it involved more people in the translation decisions, which was a good thing for local ownership of the translation.

CHAPTER FOURTEEN

ACQUIRING NEW PETS

While Csaba was acquiring words, we, back at the ol'
homestead, were acquiring new pets.

We have had many African animals given to us as
pets. How these animals came into our possession, how
they adapted, and their unique quirks made life not
only interesting, but a lot of fun as well. Some of my favorite pets that were a little more on the eccentric side
were the parrot, the bush baby, and the mongoose.

An African friend brought a young parrot to us one
day that had been trapped, clipped, and put into a
small cage. This bird soon made it clear that he hated
all people. When anyone went close to his cage, he

gave a warning scream. I pitied the bird and bought him for the equivalent of $10, and then Koffi became a part of our lives.

Koffi was an African Gray parrot and native to the Ivory Coast. He was also a difficult bird to befriend. Every time I got near his cage, he would scream at me until I went away. I knew it would take time to earn his trust, but I had the time. This particular kind of bird could be quite compatible with humans, and I wanted to try to bring him to that point. To help him get over his fear of people, I put the cage in the living room where he could be with us. But every time someone walked near his cage, the parrot screamed. With so much traffic in the house, he eventually got tired of screaming and soon settled for a warning growl.

After several days, he quit growling as long as we didn't get too close. I then decided to approach him up to the point where he started to feel threatened. When I reached that spot, I sat down and waited until the growling stopped, and he accepted me at that distance. Each day I would repeat the process going a little closer until I could sit right by his cage and read. He was not too happy about this, and a rumbly growl would come from the depths of his throat. Soon that stopped, as he accepted me within this range.

When I felt he was ready, I reached into his cage and handed him a peanut. He resented this intrusion and screamed at the outrage. I kept my hand there, but he would not accept the peanut. So I had to force the situation by removing his food. After a few hours I tried again with the peanut. He growled but kept looking at that peanut. Finally, he got up his courage, reached over and grabbed the peanut with extreme indignation. Then he went as far away from me as possible to eat it. I repeated this often until a wonderful thing happened: he quit growling at me. After that, he tolerated me as an inevitable part of his life. He later would learn to tolerate the whole family, and eventually, he would come to love us.

Now that the bird had accepted my presence, it was time to start handling him. I opened up the cage and let him out. He glided down, then hopped onto the floor, hiding under the couch. To get him back, I held a stick up to his breast and pushed it against him. With the pressure on his breast he stepped on the stick but then flew off again. I repeated this until I could get him to stay on the stick. When he consistently stayed on, I tilted the stick down so that he walked up the stick and onto my hand. This was a bit scary as the strength of his beak was formidable if he chose to bite. But I kept my hand very still, and he paid no attention to me.

Once he was used to my hand, I tried stroking his back. But every time I tried to touch it he would reach around to try to bite me. Finally, I diverted his attention away from my finger and lightly touched his back. Koffi didn't like this and growled. After doing this many times over the next few days, I finally was able to rest my finger longer on his back. Eventually, I was able to stroke and handle him with no problems. The last hurdle was overcome many months later when the bird gave a sign of true bonding by lowering his head and exposing his neck. I knew what to do, I reached down and scratched that neck, ruffling the feathers backwards. The bonding was now complete. From then on, we'd be scratching his neck often. He liked to come down and get scratches from Csaba as he read in the hammock. If the bird came down the wrong side and ended up at Csaba's foot, the parrot would remind him of his duty by nipping Csaba's toes.

Koffi also had a mischievous streak, and the kids had to watch out for what their stealth parrot would do next. For example, Koffi liked board games and especially the game of Monopoly. Often when the kids were deep into a game, the parrot would creep slowly down from his window perch and hop onto the floor. He would then waddle quietly over when no one was looking and grab a hotel off the board. I think he liked their red color. But when the kids spotted the thief, the parrot would dash back up to safety with his prize in his beak. No matter how hard the kids tried, they couldn't get their hotel back. So the bird would spend the rest of his time in peace trying to crack the hotel open to see what kind of nut was inside. This got to be a bit of a nuisance as playing pieces would be pinched by the parrot and rendered out of commission for the rest of the game. The kids finally learned that when they wanted to play any board game at all, they had to confine the parrot to his cage.

Then there were times when the parrot could prove to be quite the annoyance. One time in particular, there was a cold going around the family and Andreas had it pretty bad. He kept making uncouth snorting sounds. After a few days, he seemed to have gotten better but then we heard him at it again, but this time he was being a bit excessive in his snorting and coughing. Csaba reprimanded Andreas, but he pleaded innocence. Sure enough, it was the bird who had learned how to cough, snort and clear his throat too. We could hardly wait for that one to leave his recall memory.

But soon enough, an animal that couldn't talk, snort, or steal hotels off Park Place made an appearance into our family, almost by mistake.

THE BUSHBABY

I was out in our yard when some Bakwé children greeted me. They had what looked like a mouse tied on the end of a string by its waist, and they swung the poor creature around like a yo-yo. I felt sorry for whatever it was and asked to have it, out of pity, even if it was only a mouse. They handed the animal over to me, and then I noticed it wasn't a mouse at all. It was a miniature bushbaby, which is really a dwarf galago, a member of the nocturnal lesser primates. He looked like a miniature monkey with a bottle brush tail, and he stood only three inches tall. His face was built for the night with huge nocturnal eyes that engulfed his tiny face. Since he was an insectivore, he had light, delicate ears that could turn and twist in minute movements to locate an insect.

He was so exhausted by their rough play that he clung pitifully to my thumb and soon fell fast asleep from fatigue. I thought we would lose him since he was so weak, but I gave him some milk, and he regained strength. After a few days he was able to eat fruit and insects, which he loved. We made a little wooden house and set it up high in his cage, and then added a swing and a bell for him to play with.

In the evening, he was quite sociable and loved to go for a romp when I let him out. Since his hind legs were meant for springing, they were disproportionately long for his tiny body, reminding us of furry frog's legs. He liked to make his rounds by jumping from person to person, then onto the window, then over to the couch, and then back on us again. A couple of times we almost lost him in the curtains because he was so small. Yet, for being only three inches tall, he could span a good six feet with his jumps.

But his love of play could be an annoyance too. One night I woke up to a bell ringing and a swing banging. I got up and looked into his cage, and the bushbaby stared at me with his huge nocturnal eyes begging me to play. Not wanting to play at one o'clock in the morning, I turned over to go back to sleep. This was useless because he continued to play with his swing and bell. To make him stop, I had to take his toys away from him. He then went hopping noiselessly around his cage as I drifted back to sleep.

The next day when I took him out to play, I was met by a grumpy bush baby who acted as if it was still in the middle of the night (which it was for him). But, since I was not nocturnal and wanted to enjoy him when I could see, I sometimes took him out during the day. This didn't go over too well with His Grumpiness. When disturbed in so untimely a manner, he would come out sleepily from his wooden house, stand up to his full three-inch height and act like a miniature King

Kong, all but beating his breast in rage, roaring in that squeaky way of his. I couldn't blame him; I knew what it was like to be woken up in the middle of the night by someone wanting to play.

MONGOOSE AND GREED

If the bushbaby was playful and the parrot mischievous, the mongoose was both. Not only that, but mongooses are notorious for their greed, which brought the most fun of all.

I once had two mongooses that I referred to as husband and wife due to their similarities to a cranky old married couple. Since mongooses loved lizards, one day I took a dead lizard and tossed it into their cage. The wife got there first and sank her teeth deep into it. Knowing that her dear husband would want to have his share, she quickly turned her furry rump towards him adding many growls for emphasis. This did not meet with her husband's idea of wifely submission, so he bit her on the behind. At this insult, the wife took off with the lizard in her mouth and darted around the cage with her darling husband close behind. Mongoose oaths were growled out and general confusion ensued as the two chased each other around the cage.

Since it didn't look like it was going to end anytime soon, I dropped in a second lizard in the cage. The wife, being quicker than her partner, dashed in and somehow managed to get it into her mouth as well. Her husband, now enraged at this second affront, chased her with more vigor around the confines of the cage hoping desperately to share in one of her prizes. I laughed at this spectacle and dropped in a third lizard. Guess what happened?

The wife, still full of spunk and ginger, lunged at the third dead lizard and tried to get it into her mouth as well. She did not want her husband to get any. Well, she was unsuccessful and all three came tumbling out of her mouth. She was then chased by an indignant husband who still didn't know she was without lizard. Eventually the couple caught on that the chase was fruitless and sniffed out the dropped lizards on the floor, each picking up one and taking it into a corner to eat. They then had their ritual meal, with their furry rumps blocking each other out just in case. From each corner, the emitting of an occasional mongoose oath could be heard to solidify the unity that this loving couple felt over their fine meal.

Over the years, we have had other unusual pets, such as a chameleon that sat on the shutters looking like a small green gargoyle chiseled in stone. He followed the kids around the room with his little volcanic eyes. The problem with him was that we kept losing him when he changed color and blended into objects around the room.

The other notable pet was Richard, the little forest deer that was the size of a large chicken and quite the connoisseur. He was very hard to feed because he liked only rose and hibiscus petals, leaves off of one species of ornamental bush, peanuts, bread, a few wild nuts, cape cherries, and imported pears. We were thankful for all these animals, and we reveled in the variety and spice these exotic creatures brought into our daily lives. It made our village home a much more interesting place to live.

CHAPTER FIFTEEN

SKY-KILLED-COW AND OTHER UNIQUE WORDS

When you are in a different culture and studying the language, you can stumble across some pretty fascinating ways of saying things. I mean, would it be odd if someone said to you "I love you with all my liver?" or if you got a candied liver for Valentine's day?

Csaba found out that the word *liver* was a powerful Bakwé word that was used in the place of *heart* in our language. According to the Bakwé, the liver was the seat of emotions instead of the heart. Certain Bakwé terms used the word *liver* in them. To have faith in God was *to lean your liver upon God*. To have hope was *to lay down your liver upon something*. The word *Mercy* was *to have pity-liver*. The word *Patience* was translated as *liver fall fall*. So, if you tell a person to be patient you are saying to them, *to let your liver (emotions) fall down.*

Color provided some intriguing insights, since Csaba found that there weren't many words describing colors which made translating certain passages a bit of a challenge. The Bakwé have words for *black, white, red, yellow,* and *green.* The word for *red* was the same word for *ripe.* The word for *green* used the word *leaf* in it. They had a word for *blue,* called *plu,* but it actually was a loan word that came from English that was acquired during the time the English were trading off the coast. So how did the Bakwé describe the other colors?

Csaba found out that the color purple, depending on the shade, could be called either *blue, red* or *black.* All dark colors were *black.* So, a dark navy blue, purple, dark gray and brown would all be named *black* as well. The color orange was called either *red* or *yellow* depending on the hue. The color *pink* was just called *red.*

What was odd to us was that they didn't consider the sky blue. This was probably because they didn't consider that it even had a color. Clouds were either white or black depending on the weather. And all the shades in between? That was anyone's guess.

So, how did Csaba translate Revelation 17:4, where it says, "The woman was arrayed in purple and scarlet . . . "?

The two colors were close, but purple was darker than red, so he translated it: "The woman was arrayed in red and bright red."

In any culture, how things are named shows how they value those things. Take vegetation for example. In America, there are hundreds of names for all sorts of ornamental bushes, flowers, roses and grasses, but in Bakwé this is not the case. There is a generic name for *tree* but nothing special for the generic word *bush*. So, a bush was just *a little tree*. There were specific names for the trees that were important to them like those used for medicine or the hardwoods sold for commerce, but specific names for the numerous trees in the tropical forest were lacking.

The grasses didn't even fare as well as the trees. There were no special words for any type of *grass*. Since the people liked a cleaned area in front of their house with no vegetation, grass was considered a weed. In fact, the Bakwé word *sipi* was used for *weed, herb,* and *grass,* all of which must be cleared off and thrown away.

Flowers had an engaging name. They were called *a shine-shine-thing.*

So, in James 1:11, the literal Bakwé read something like this: "As the sun rises and heats/dries the weeds (grass), its *shine-shine-thing* (flower) falls . . . ."

Animals that are pets also didn't fare too well in the line-up of importance. The generic word for animal was just *meat*. So, if you had a pet deer, you had a *pet meat* which didn't bode well for the deer. This was the most common way of saying things, though some animals had their own names as well.

Some words were real puzzlers as to how they came about since no one knew. The word for *perseverance* was *scratching inside you*. But the most unique word was *rainbow* which in Bakwé literally meant *sky-killed-cow*. Csaba was curious about how they came up with that term but nobody could tell him; he could only surmise. Could the killing of a cow represent the idea of a sacrifice that went along with a covenant? Who knew? But stumbling across these things made being a language detective so much fun.

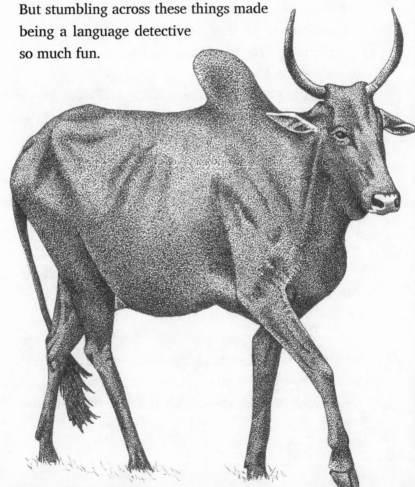

CHAPTER SIXTEEN

PEREZ'S WEDDING

Perez, our literacy supervisor, was to be married, and we had the privilege of attending the wedding. There were to be three ceremonies on the chosen weekend. The first one would be the civil ceremony before a government official during the day. That night there would be a feast with singing from a few invited choirs and a message from the Harrist priest, since Perez was a Harrist. The day after, on Sunday, would be the church wedding with the actual vows.

The civil ceremony came and went with no problem. The next stage of the wedding was something else. At the feast, it soon became apparent that the choirs were not in high spirits. Perez, in his exuberance, asked not one, but three visiting choirs to come from other Harrist churches down the road. Somehow, due to a slight oversight, they lacked a singing schedule, so no one quite knew when to sing. It was left up to the choirs to decide. Since they all decided that they should be first, it looked like the competition of the choirs was about to begin.

So, one choir started singing while the others fumed. When the first choir eventually stopped, the second group grabbed the spotlight, much to the chagrin of the third. When the second choir finally got tired and stopped, the third choir refused to sing because they were too upset at being snubbed by the insult of being last. Hot words were exchanged in the confusion of it all, and at the end of this volley, no choirs sang because they *all* were offended. At this point someone tried to get the intercom music going to fill in the gaps of the dead space. This only produced squeaks and screeches that made us wince because the PA system wasn't working either. We listened to a bit of screeching until thankfully one of the choirs began singing again. We were all relieved.

After the singing came a series of speeches by a Harrist official from Abidjan. Then came the cutting of the wedding cake. Since no one in our village had any experience with wedding cakes, I had been recruited. My attempt at the cake was a disaster. What happened? I had taken the cake out of the freezer and didn't let it dethaw before I iced it (cake decorator's sin number one).

On top of that I had forgotten the icing recipe and added too much milk (cake decorator's sin number two). The result was a waterfall of icing off the side of the cake on the day of the wedding! I would have sat there in a pool of sweat and discouragement had not our personnel director, Ann, been visiting us at that moment with her son and his wife who had come in from England. Ann and her daughter-in-law knew cakes and how to decorate, so I gladly turned it over to them. They somehow miraculously salvaged the wreck and made it into something beautiful with roses, little puffed stars and silver balls. I was impressed. At the ceremony, the beautiful cake was cut and served to all the guests and was much appreciated. They passed out pieces to everyone, and they served cake to us three times.

After this the dancing began. As people piled into the aisles to dance, I saw Alexis' wife, Marie, holding Sophie's baby while Sophie danced to her heart's content. (You'll remember Sophie as the singer in the Bakwé church service in chapter 4.) Sophie's baby looked so cute in her ruffled finery that I wanted to hold her. I held up my arms towards the baby and she was instantly placed in my lap. Once I had my prize sitting there, I looked at her and smiled. She was a very pretty baby with light, coffee-colored skin and two little chocolate drops for eyes, chocolate drops that stared intently at my face, studying it. As the baby gave me a thorough going over, I noticed that she had become deadly silent and perplexed. I got the feeling that I was not passing muster. To her, somehow, something was drastically wrong. She was trying to figure out why my face was washed of that rich, dark hue that she was so used to. Yet, she showed no fear, just amazement.

As I talked to her in English with the little nothings that are so commonly said to people of her age, her astonishment grew since my voice lacked the melodic tones of her mother tongue. Her little chocolate eyes hardly left my face. Pretty soon her lip curled under, and she started to whimper. I looked around for her guardian in that laughing, dancing crowd but Marie was nowhere to be seen. I could see her mama, Sophie, out there hooting and hollering in full swing, yet she was not within shouting range either. No, mama would not be available until much later. The baby continued to fix her little perplexed eyes on me and cry softly. What was I to do? I couldn't change my skin; the baby would just have to wait. Eventually Marie returned and the baby went back to her old familiar world where everyone was the same color and spoke the same language. We then left the crowd to await the next day's happenings.

The next day most everyone showed up at the village's Harrist church dressed up in the standard white. The priests were also in white except that they had a black sash wound around their chest in the shape of a cross. It had quite the effect: a church full of people clothed in all white with dark faces except the front row where the guests had dark clothes and white faces (us) and a few Africans from other churches with their brightly colored African cloth. The service started with singing from the choirs who all seemed to be in fellowship again. When the Harrists sang they didn't use drums but gourds with a network of cowry shells woven around them. These were shaken to an intricate beat that could almost blow your ear drums out if you were sitting right in front of them, which we were. After the singing ended, the vows were given followed by an admonition from the head priest.

When the service was over, we all filed out in a procession along the dirt roads with the priests and the married couple in front, the honored guests coming next, followed by the choir, and everyone else in the rear. The whole group walked and sang the whole length of the village. Perez, who normally led the choir, was walking in front where he was supposed to be with his bride, but all too soon he broke rank to go back to his old position as leader of the choir once more. He was obviously in his element again. His new wife didn't seem to mind as she was too busy dancing to the thundering rattles to care.

The day after the wedding, they came by to visit and thanked us for all our work behind the scenes. I asked Perez if all his guests had departed. He said, "No they haven't. They are sleeping all over our floors, in the living room, and even in our bedroom." Evidently when the arrangements were made as to who was to sleep where, they forgot to make room for the new couple.

In learning about the customs of the people around us, we gained an understanding of some of the difficulties they faced when trying to get married. Here were some of the stories we heard.

One young man was in hot trouble. He was by nature impetuous and fiery. He knew what he wanted and was always in a hurry to get it. This time he had finally found Miss Right and was anxious to get on with the wedding. He asked her to marry him. So far so good. The starstruck lover then went to the pastor to find a date to do the wedding. When he couldn't get the date he wanted, he suggested doing the wedding sooner than planned and the pastor agreed. But guess what? He forgot the minor detail of asking his fiancée if this date would be suitable to her. So, he wrote the invitations and sent them out to everybody. He even was thoughtful enough to send one to his fiancée. She received the invitation to her wedding and became quite upset when she realized that she couldn't be there that day. Too bad!

So, she went to the Pastor and wanted to know what was going on. The Pastor was surprised to find out that she didn't know what was going on. Mr. Impetuous was now in deep trouble. Since this was Africa and getting information out takes time, there was no way to stop everyone from showing up anyhow to a wedding that the bride couldn't be at. When the guests arrived, they were met by a very disillusioned groom and an embarrassed Pastor who told them that there would be no wedding since the bride couldn't make it that day—sorry. I think this marriage was off to a bad start (actually it never took place).

Are weddings times of joy and happiness, or heartache and frustration? When a wedding is imminent, nothing can be assumed. A local pastor in a town near us was scheduled to do premarital counseling for an engaged couple from an ethnic group other than Bakwé. The pastor greeted the future wife by saying, "So you're the happy bride-to-be!" The girl retorted hotly with, "Oh, I'm not happy. I don't even want to marry this guy!" On further questioning, he found out that she wasn't even asked whether she wanted to be a bride. She was just simply told by her father that it was already arranged, and that she would be in the wedding, like it or not.

We had experience with this particular custom when we hired a girl from a northern ethnic group to help Janvier temporarily in the kitchen. She couldn't have been over sixteen years old at the time. When she didn't show up one morning, Janvier went to inquire where she was. He found out she had been told that morning by her mother that she was to marry a man thirty years her senior and would become wife number four. She was not asked her opinion, and to resist in that culture would have been social and economic suicide for her. She could not live in isolation from the very people she depended on for her survival. Janvier and his brother were somber that day pitying her rather dismal plight.

Even though arranged marriages still happened, the majority of the attachments that we knew were by choice. When asked how the Bakwé did it, we were told that if you saw a girl from another village who pleased you, then you asked her to come home with you to your village. When her father found out that his daughter was missing, he would ask around trying to find out where she went. You may send a message that you had his daughter. But if you did, then the father would ask the uncomfortable question of how and when you were to pay the dowry. If you didn't pay the bride dowry, he would want her sent back. You might decide not to do that either. This could make him even madder, but eventually he'd calm down. If she gave you several children, then you could always pay the dowry later to ensure that the children would remain yours after you died and would not go back to her parents. If she didn't give you children, then she could always leave, and then you could find someone else.

Csaba thought this little arrangement was less than ideal, so he gave a Bible study for his Bakwé colleagues on how to gain a wife. All of our men sought their wives, and asked permission from their fathers first before they took them, and it was a joy to see them get married.

CHAPTER SEVENTEEN

OUT OF DEATH'S JAWS

Some of the most important key words in the Bible were some of the most challenging to find words for in Bakwé. Here are a few:

> *Holy Spirit:* The word for *holy* was a difficult one to agree upon. Some wanted to use the word *-pötı* which was used for water that was clear and calm, not disturbed. It also had the connotation of peaceful. Some languages will use white or clean for the idea of pure or holy. What they finally agreed upon was a compound word using *'nyüna* which literally means *good-color* or *pure,* and *-Susu* which means

135

spirit. So *Holy Spirit* in Bakwé is *Nyüna -Susu, the pure spirit.*

Lord: The Bakwé never had a kingdom. The largest unit of authority they had traditionally known was the patri-clan which was two or three generations descending from a common male ancestor. As a result, they had no concept of sovereigns or lords, so coming up with a word for Lord was a challenge. Using *chief* was a possibility, but the word *chief* in Bakwé was a loan word, and they wanted to find a real Bakwé word.

For a time, they tried the word *'Wʋsinyɔɔ,* which literally meant *Most high person.* But later on, they found a rarely used word, *'Pläkänyɔɔ,* that had more the sense of a sovereign. It literally meant *World-owner-person.*

Kingdom; kingdom of God: In translating into Bakwé, it was often difficult to find an exact word that communicated the full breadth of a concept. For example, finding a satisfactory word for *kingdom* as in *kingdom of God,* was quite the challenge. The term in the Greek included the idea of the authority of a king, his rule or reign, and subjects who were cared for and protected by the king. The Bakwé head of family exercised authority only over his courtyard, which included the houses and the people in it. So for the verse "God's Kingdom has come among you" they tried "God's court-yard-rule has come among you."

It worked, sort of, because God was very big and His courtyard encompassed the world, but it still seemed way too small a word. After some months of translating it this way, they finally settled on *God's world-rule* which communicated both authority, reign, and the relationship of a ruler and subjects. Unlike the first term, it was also all-encompassing in scope and size.

Savior: The word *Savior* was an interesting one. They settled on the literal phrase *out of the mouth of something bad-take out person.* This something bad was just understood that you needed saving from it. For example, if a leopard has you in its teeth, then the person who takes you out of its mouth is your savior. This phrase worked because when you expanded this concept out to the human race, we are all in the jaws of death, condemned to die an eternal death due to our rebellion against God. It took the giving of a Savior

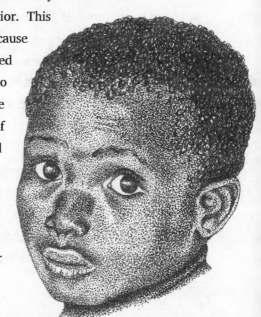

through God's Son Jesus Christ to pay the penalty for our sins by his death on the cross, take us out of the jaws of death, and bring us into eternal life with Him. That is a Savior, and He is Jesus Christ.

MARTIN COMES HOME

We saw a lot of the hard effects of sin in the village. There were deaths due to AIDS. There were poisonings due to retaliations of aggrieved neighbors. There were also the unseen deaths through women having abortions. It sped us on to the urgency of what we were doing, bringing the Word of God to them so that they could be taken out of the jaws of the death and brought into life eternal.

Our family was at the table finishing breakfast when in popped the familiar figures of our two helpers, Janvier and Bibionay. They greeted us and then went to their morning's work of starting the fire and heating the water for dishes. Not long after, another shadow came creeping in with a hat. He silently sat down by the door.

Csaba greeted him with a chuckle. "Monsieur Le chapeau (Mr. Hat), how are you doing this fine morning? I would never have recognized you without your cap on."

Martin's face slowly spread into a wide grin. It was a characteristic grin that always poked out from under his baseball cap which he was rarely seen without. He spoke a greeting in return, then continued to wait for his cup of coffee if Janvier remembered him in the bustle. Martin was Janvier's younger cousin who had accompanied him down from Burkina to find work in Ivory Coast.

Since Janvier wanted to raise chickens for sale, Martin was to be the labor while Janvier would furnish the brains and the capital. This part of the arrangement worked well for a while until, like an unruly teenager, Martin began to get obstinate. He didn't like the work and did it grudgingly. He stayed out late in town and would get into trouble. Janvier counseled him again and again in the ways of the Lord telling him that if he continued on like this, he would ruin his life and that there were many men who chased after women and would slowly get sick and die. He must turn his life over to God.

This was not what Martin wanted to hear. He wanted to be master of his own life, and to show this, he decided to break with Janvier and to go out on his own. Janvier tried to persuade him to stay because, after all, Martin was under Janvier's guardianship and protection. What would he tell his parents? But Martin was not to be dissuaded and left in contempt of Janvier's position as older brother.

So Martin left to live the wild way he wanted to live, which was not according to God's way. After this, Janvier heard about his cousin's life and was distressed to see how he was living. Janvier kept praying for him, hoping he would return to God's ways, and during that time, Martin popped in and out of Janvier's life. A period of a year went by while we were on furlough. After we came back, we found out that Martin was quite sick and needed help. In fact, it had been months in coming. At first it was a little here and a little there until the period of sickness grew longer and longer. Pretty soon he was losing weight and getting weaker until there were no periods of relief. He couldn't work anymore and soon didn't have money so he could eat. All his friends from his wild days had left him and he was hurting. He decided to come back to the only home that he knew. He came back to Janvier and asked his forgiveness. Janvier welcomed him in once more.

He was now regularly hanging out at our place again. As always, Csaba would give him a cheerful, teasing greeting and Martin would respond with his characteristic big smile which came now from a very gaunt face under a way too big hat. But this time was different because Csaba got involved in a deeper way. Csaba talked to Martin about the Lord and told him that he was on a cliff, at the edge of hell. There was still time to turn around before he fell in. His time could be short so he should not play around with his life anymore. He needed to look to the Savior, Jesus Christ, who was there with outstretched arms, willing to receive him if he should turn, repent and believe. Martin could not make it without Christ doing it all—nobody can.

Martin looked down while Csaba was talking and said that he understood and would think on it. In the meantime, after talking with Janvier, we decided to send Martin back to Burkina to go to a hospital that was closer to his family and village. As Martin left, we prayed that he would respond to that call and truly go to a home that could only be found in Christ. A home where there are no more tears, suffering, or pain, where pardoned sinners rest and joyful songs are rendered up to our Lord and Savior in a final resting place—heaven.

(Not long after that, we got word that Martin had died. We didn't know if he responded to the gospel but hoped that he had repented and turned to God.)

ABORTION—A LESSON FROM A GOAT FETUS

The other hard effect of sin, abortion, was not really common in our area since most women wanted their children. But, with the breaking up of society, some young women were doing abortions on themselves to keep their lives of ease and harlotry. This was sad, but what was amazing was how the Bakwé society viewed abortion, which was very different from our own society.

One day a woman became pregnant by a man from another ethnic group, out of wedlock. The man, being married to someone else, pressured her to get an abortion, which she tried, using herbs. The elders of the village found out about it and were furious. They brought the man to trial for attempted murder. Because he was from a neighboring ethnic group, they accused him of wanting to spill Bakwé blood, which was a very serious offense, especially if you had an alliance with the Bakwé. The man was told that if the baby died, he would have to go through the trial for murder. If the child lived, he would have to pay all bills for the birth, then support the child through life which was a heavy fine indeed. Thankfully the child lived.

But the young women of the village still did abortions secretly when they did not want their children, thinking they could just get rid of their problem before it came to light. And in an odd twist of events, God would use my science lab in a very powerful way to address this horrific sin.

One day Janvier went to the market to get some goat organs for me to use. Buying the goat organs served a double purpose. I liked giving the biology lesson with hands-on material and Janvier liked eating it afterwards. It was amazing what people considered edible in the village—eyes, head, brains, guts, you name it, but to each his own. Anyhow, what was intriguing on occasion was that the butcher threw in something extra as a bonus. This time it was a uterus with twin goats inside. The female goat marked for slaughter had been pregnant but was too early to show. This saddened us some, but it had an even greater effect on Janvier. He was amazed to see two perfectly formed little goats about three inches long with ears, eyes, legs and even tiny hooves. They were fascinating.

I told Janvier that the human babies were also miniatures of the real thing inside the uterus even though the mother didn't show until later. I explained that people often did abortions when the child was small but still perfectly formed. They called the child a fetus and said it was not a person yet. Janvier looked at me with this incredibly pained expression, as though he wanted to cry. As I held these perfectly formed little goats with hooves, ears and eyes, Janvier cried out, "That's not a potential goat! That is a real goat and when the women do their abortions, they are killing real people and not potential ones! I keep preaching to these girls to turn away from their sin with their lovers, but they don't pay me any attention. Now I can show that they have committed murder as well!" Then he took the baby goats and stormed out of the kitchen.

He went into the village and found some of the girls, and then showed them the baby goats. He said, "These goats are what a human baby would be at this stage. They are perfectly formed within the womb even though the mother doesn't show yet. When you do your abortions, you are killing a real baby and not a potential one. You are committing murder and God will hold it against you at judgment day. He will not allow you into His presence with your blood guilt on your hands. The only way out of this awful mess is to accept the gift of Jesus Christ dying on the cross to pay the penalty for your sins, through Christ's own precious blood. This blood will wash away your awful sins and make you clean again, removing your guilt."

Instead of the mocking grins and cutting remarks that Janvier usually received from them, the girls reacted with some emotion. One girl ran away crying. Just about all of them were in tears. No one passed it off lightly. I guess my science project had a far more reaching impact than I had originally intended.

CHAPTER EIGHTEEN

JANVIER'S TESTIMONY

How did Janvier get like this? Why was he so bold in championing the helpless? It came from when he was a child and suffered severe neglect, abandonment, and abuse. It also came from overcoming his past with the strength of God and then going on to minister, not only to the ones who had abused him, but to all people in need, which included the unborn.

Janvier was born in Burkina Faso to a chief, the head of a clan. His mother was the youngest of his father's three wives. When his father died, his mother was obligated to marry again, then forced to leave her very young son behind with the clan. He was taken care of by his father's first wife, who was like a grandma to him. Life was good as long as she was alive, but when he was five years old, she died. He was then left in the hands of the other relatives who didn't care for him so well. There were just so many mouths to feed and his was one too many. Life was very hard for him because they treated him like a slave and abused him in many ways. They forced him to work at that young age, and he was only served one meal a day in the evening because he didn't have a mother to watch out for him.

Lack of food was always an ongoing problem, and in order to gain the needed nourishment, he had to work for it in the fields along with other members of the extended family. But Janvier was treated differently. While still only a little guy, after a hard day's work completing his portion, he would leave to go back to eat with the others, but would be told that he needed to do extra work if he wanted to eat. Even after he worked an extra portion, there was sometimes not much food left for him after the others ate. Other times they said he could only eat after he insulted himself, so that they could have fun at his expense. He would do as they said because he was so hungry. If there was no food left, he would steal. Sometimes he would go out in the fields and tunnel through the ground under a yam hill and would cut the yams off from underneath so that no one would notice. In this way he survived, yet life continued to be very tough, and he felt that no one loved him.

One day around the age of ten, he found a Catholic church in a nearby town. He went in and saw a cross with a figure of a man on it. This man looked so compassionate and loving that Janvier kept looking at it. The priest came up to him and said that this was Jesus who died for him. Janvier wondered why this Jesus would die for him? But it touched his hurting heart so deeply that he decided to go to the Catholic church to find out what it all meant. Yet, in order to attend the church, he had to do extra work on Saturdays. After this, he was allowed to go to church on Sundays. But he still suffered at the hands of his family because they withheld food from him after he got back from church. On Monday they would punish him again by giving him double work.

One day after working the fields, one of his aunts said he could have a yam to eat that was roasting in the fire. When his uncle saw him take it, he assumed that he had stolen it. So, the uncle took another hot yam fresh from the fire, jammed it in Janvier's mouth and held his mouth shut so that the hot yam burned deep into his tongue. The wound was so severe that he couldn't eat for a week. Other things happened to him as well, like the time he was hit with an ax on his head, and everyone thought he was dead. But an aunt took him to the hospital, and he lived.

When the abuse at home got so bad, Janvier ran to different hideouts that he had made. He would make a cave in the side of a hill and cover it over with brush so that nobody would know the entrance was even there, and then he would spend the night in that place. He learned to fend for himself in other ways as well. Since one of his jobs was as a herder for the family's cows, he would milk them and drink the milk with millet he had gleaned from the fields. He would also find wild bee-hives and eat their honey. He killed lizards and snakes and ate their meat. He didn't say if he had cooked it or not, but that was how he survived as a child. He would even lose himself for up to three months traveling with the cows out in the wilderness and people wondered where he went. But still, he couldn't live forever in the outback and eventually he would come back. But when he did, he felt that there was no one there who loved him, since he didn't have a mother.

There came a time, at the age of thirteen, when he felt that life in his village was no longer tolerable, and that if he stayed, his life would be in danger. He decided it was time for him to leave once and for all. He seized his opportunity when a truck stopped near the village. Janvier hopped in and hid himself in the back under a sack. The driver took off and arrived in a large city. But Janvier had nowhere to go after that and had no possessions, only the pair of shorts he was wear-ing and nothing else, not even a shirt on his back. An older woman saw him and found out that he needed a place to live, so she said he could stay and work for her. She was kind to him and treated him like a son. He started cooking for her, and she was surprised he knew how, but he had learned by just watching others. Life continued to be good for him until she moved on to another city. He decided that he needed to move on too and went down to Ivory Coast where there were more job opportunities.

When he got to Ivory Coast, he didn't know anyone there either, so he went to a cook shop and helped the woman in exchange for food and a place to sleep at night, even if it was outside on the benches. Somehow or other, after much time working at different jobs, he worked up the ladder and ended up in some good positions as a cook. But through all this, he still didn't know why the kind, suffering Jesus, that he had seen on the cross at the Catholic church, had died for him. That knowledge was soon to come.

There was a man who was a Christian that knew that Janvier was Catholic. He said to Janvier, "I see you are religious, but do you know Jesus?" When Janvier said that he did not, the man invited him to go to church with him. Janvier went and heard the gospel of how that suffering Jesus really loved him and died for his sins to save him from hell. Janvier finally understood now why Jesus came to die for him and that God's saving grace could be his too. He accepted Christ and His gift of love that was offered to him so freely. That night he dreamed he was climbing up from a deep chasm. As he climbed, Jesus reached down to take His hand and pulled him up out of the hole. At the top, Janvier saw a lot of sheep on one side, and a lot of food on the other. Jesus said to him, "Give food to the sheep." From one who had suffered such a lack of food in his life Janvier was now bid to give out of the abundance of food that Jesus offered to other spiritually hungry people.

After this, Janvier became bold in his faith and proclaimed it to people, even to witchdoctors. They would try to hex him, but Janvier would just laugh and say that they couldn't kill him through their sorcery. Jesus was more powerful than them and would protect him. His preaching had a powerful effect on people and many converted. He met us after he came to Soubré when we were living there waiting for our village house to be built. Csaba was so impressed by his faith and good character that he asked him to work for us as our cook.

When we moved to the village, he became an integral part of our work, helping not only with the running of the kitchen but also in praying, evangelizing, and preaching to the Bakwé and others as well. He always had a compassion for people, especially the ones who were the neediest, like children who were either abandoned or needed help. After he worked for us for some years, he finally got enough money to go back to Burkina Faso to visit his old village, the one he had fled from so many years before. When he arrived in his home village, he gave them gifts from Ivory Coast and told them he didn't hold anything against them since he was now a Christian. The women were ashamed and cried, knowing how badly they had treated him.

Over the coming years when he would visit his relations, he would pray for them when they were sick, and he would preach to them about Jesus, and some became Christians. Janvier even had a hand in helping get a church started there and was now in a position to continually do them good. And the boy who had been chased away by their abuse was now the very one who had come back to do them good. Christ's salvation and healing had swallowed up the bitterness of the cruelty he had experienced, because Christ reigned in his life.

He said that he would not be the person he was today if he hadn't suffered like that. It formed him, but in a good way. And God protected him throughout. Though he suffered severely, he thanks God for it all now because that is the main reason he has been a help to so many people, both children and adults, wanting them to know the love of this amazing Jesus. And what about the mother that had left him at so young an age? He had prayed for his mother's salvation for years, and on her death bed, she had received Jesus before she died.

CHAPTER NINETEEN

PUZZLES

Csaba ran into difficulty when trying to translate the words for the number 144,000 in Revelation. This would not have been a problem if the passage had just used the numerals, but instead, it had to be spelled out. The reason for the difficulty was that the Bakwé rarely had to count anything over a thousand. What complicated things even more was that there were two methods of counting, one for money, and the other for people and things.

In their system for people, you count by ones up to five with each number having a name. When you get beyond that, you start adding. The number for 8 when using words is 5 + 3 people. When you get to 10 there is a separate word for that. After this you start adding again. So, 18 would be in words, $10 + 5 + 3$ people. Once you hit 20 there is a separate word for that which you now use as your base for adding and multiplying. So, 40 is two 20s, or to make it simpler I'll use the times symbol for 2×20. The number 57 sounded out would be $2 \times 20 + 10 + 5 + 2$. This adding and multiplying will go all the way up to 400 where there is another base word used. For example, 4,000 is 10×400s.

So, back in the translation, 144,000 people in Bakwé was spelled out literally as $[(10 \times 20) \times 400] + [(8 \times 20) \times 400]$ people, which equaled 144,000.

So, the way they translated Revelation 14:1 was, "Then I looked, and behold, a Lamb standing on Mount Zion, and with Him people of ten twenties four hundred, and people of eight twenties four hundred (144,000) having His Father's name written on their foreheads." Since people were not used to counting this high, and to keep the text from getting really confusing, we included the number (144,000) in parentheses in the translation to make it simpler to read.

Metaphors were also a puzzler. In the following examples, to keep the exact metaphor would be to lose the meaning of the text completely.

Luke 1:42 says "'Blessed are you among women, and blessed is the fruit of your womb!'" Unfortunately, in Bakwé, the phrase *fruit of the womb* means a tumor that makes you sick, like cancer. Translating this literally would mean "Blessed are you among women and blessed is *your cancer.*" This literal translation would give the exact opposite meaning from what the text was trying to say, so they had to translate it this way instead: "Blessed is the child you will give birth to."

Another example of a difficult metaphor to translate is Luke 13:32 which says, "Go tell that Fox . . . ," speaking of Herod. The Bakwé don't know what a fox is, and neither do they know what it symbolizes. It would make as much sense to them as this phrase does to us, "Go tell that hedgehog . . ."

Different cultures use different animals to symbolize things. It is common in West African folktales to have Spider be the cunning hero of the story. In Bakwé society, Rat and Hare are known for their cun-

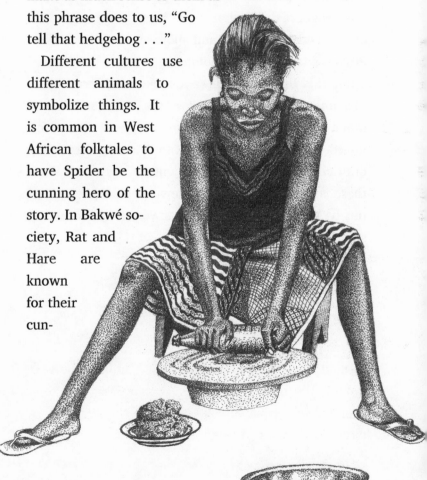

ning and wisdom which is opposite from western culture which uses Rat as the villain. But, since the Greek text used the word fox, the team didn't want to substitute it for another animal. So, they translated the verse as "Go tell that crafty-man . . ." and then put a footnote at the bottom of the page telling the reader that the Greek used the word *fox* which was a dog-like wild animal known for its craftiness and cunning.

As far as puzzles to unravel, poetry is probably the hardest genre to translate. Poetry can be found in much of the Old Testament, and more notably in Psalms, Proverbs, and Song of Solomon. Poetry is structured differently than prose. Its style includes different types of parallelism, repetition of words, and varied word order. The normal rules of grammar aren't always followed with conjunctions and other words often being omitted, which makes it difficult to translate. Then there is the fact that the Hebrew rules for poetry may not be the same for that as Bakwé poetry, so understanding both is necessary.

CHAPTER TWENTY

THE DRUNKEN WHISTLE

While Csaba worked on his puzzles in the translation, I was working on my own puzzles, still trying to figure out who was that drunken man that kept whistling in the back of our property and then always vanished when we came out?

I heard a whistle-like song coming from the bush. I stopped to listen because it sounded like it was coming from a man who was tipsy and off key. Drunken men whistling in the back of our property were not tolerable, so I decided to check it out and tell the chap to move on. Yet, when I reached the spot of my supposed drunken man, the whistle evaporated. There was only silence until I heard the whistle a little farther off in a deeper part of the bush. I stole near that spot only to find nothing and silence again. But when I saw the place where the whistle had sounded, it was a place which no man could penetrate. I then realized I was dealing with a bird and not a human, yet none of us had ever seen that bird since it loved dark, overgrown places. Try as I might, every time I tried to track down that sound, it kept evaporating.

One day I decided to walk in the wild section of our property and stopped when I got to a clump of bamboo. The stalks sprang up in thick columns to form a dark green wall that towered over a thick mat of tangled brush underneath. I was admiring the quiet wildness of this place when I saw movement in the heavy brush just beyond where I stood. I went over to investigate and found my daughter lying on the ground, very much hidden. She was in the only clear area at the bottom of the brush before the tangle started. It looked peaceful down there where the sprinkles of light from above dotted the forest floor below like paint on a dark canvas. A few sprinkles even found their way onto my daughter, who was lying low staring at something.

I bent down and followed her gaze deep into the shadows and saw a small, dark object perched on a low limb. I stood there fascinated, watching it until its voice broke the silence with that same drunken, off-key whistle that I had heard before. It was that bird that I could never see! Soon all became quiet again except for a few dewdrops that were on their way down from leafy cups above to the damp earth beneath.

The whistle broke out again, but this time it was not the bird. It was my daughter talking back to it in that same clear, off-key way. The bird moved a little closer to investigate and came more clearly into view. It swelled its little brown breast and called back to Noai whistling a challenge to this new invader of his kingdom. Noai listened carefully, then repeated the bird's song and waited. Sure enough, a response came from the little king, line for line, note for note.

Then there was silence, with the drip, drip, dripping of dew upon the leaves. The bird broke that silence by recalling songs of kingfishers, bush quail, and hawks all sung from mimicking their owners. After this, a damp quiet ensued, until the drunken whistle refrain was taken up again as if in afterthought. My daughter watched this little king intently, feeling like she was the intruder and he the rightful heir to his shadowy kingdom. She gave a parting call to the little monarch, and we slipped out of his world and back into ours. As we walked away from the darkness of the bamboo, we heard a lone, off-key whistle that grew fainter with distance until it too disappeared as we entered back into the realm of the light.

As well as tracking wild birds in dark places, other activities occupied my children in the outback section of our property. For example, after harvesting our rice,

Noai, Andreas, and Jeremiah decided to make their own shelters by using the straw from the leftover rice stalks lying in the fields after harvest. When their shelters were done, I saw them going off one day with armloads of fruit and vegetables that they had collected from our property. I asked what they were doing, and Andreas said, "living off the land." In their hands was a variety of produce from our yard, along with a bundle of rice they had harvested from the rice field. I agreed with them that they probably could live off the land on our property. I guessed they were tired of the civilized life that we lead and wanted to rough it a bit in the open wilds of our rice field. That was fine with me, but I noticed that they hadn't missed a meal at our table yet. I wondered if Robinson Crusoe had it so nice. Yes, life for a missionary kid could be so good.

CHAPTER TWENTY-ONE

FUNERALS

Funerals are an important part of Bakwé society which have their own special etiquette. And oddly enough, when someone dies, you don't just announce it directly. If you are a relative in another village and your relation dies, then you will be contacted by a messenger telling you that your relation is very sick and requesting you to come soon. This news alerts the relative that their relation might be either very ill or has just passed away. They won't know until they have arrived and hear the death wail.

At the funeral, it is proper etiquette for those close to the deceased to display the proper amount of grief. This is shown by wailing or throwing yourself on the ground in despair. If you don't, the family of the deceased might think you don't care, or even worse, suspect you of causing the death somehow through sorcery or other means. So, if you don't feel like wailing, it is better to wail anyhow. Csaba often drove groups of mourners to distant funerals. In the truck, the atmosphere was often festive and joking until they arrived at the funeral where it would turn immediately to mourning, leaving Csaba to wonder.

Another important custom is to give either money, or goats, or chickens to the family to help feed the multitude that is there. Giving is obligatory, in a voluntary type of way, because if you don't give anything, you will be criticized for being stingy, and stinginess is one of the more grievous sins in Bakwé society.

One old man knew this and decided that he wanted the benefits now of the goats and chickens he would receive at his funeral because when he was dead, he couldn't enjoy them. So, he sent people to announce to his friends and family in other villages, that he had died. On the day of his supposed funeral, waves of people came, only to find the "deceased" on the other end still very much alive to greet them. The old man said, "Thank you for coming to my funeral. Now I know how you would have mourned me, and would you please leave all these things here so we can enjoy them now?" People were flabbergasted. They didn't know what to do. Should they mourn?

Another custom is that the body must not be abandoned during the funeral. The mourners must stay up all night mourning near the body until it is safely buried the next day. The Bakwé believe that the spirit of the deceased lingers around until the body is buried. Until then, the spirit is watching to see if people mourn in sincerity. And if they don't, then the spirit can do mischief against these people, especially to those who are suspected of causing the death. Since they believe that no death is natural except for the aged, someone must be blamed. How they found the guilty party in the past was interesting. The villagers would take the body rolled up in a mat for a tour around the village. The body would then supposedly lean toward the person who had killed it. This practice has since been abolished by the government since it caused no end of strife between families after accusations had been made.

Sometimes funerals were complicated, like when a member of an allied tribe had an unresolved issue with the deceased person.

At one funeral, Csaba was waiting for the final act of burying the coffin when a young man got up from the crowd and threw down a branch on the top of the coffin. Everyone became silent since the funeral could not proceed while the branch remained there. Finally, the oldest man of the village got up and shuffled slowly over to the young man who had thrown the branch. Leaning over on bended knee in a humble, beseeching way, the old man grabbed the hands of the Branch

Thrower and pleaded with him to take gifts to allow them to continue to bury their dead. In a fascinating banter, the two talked through an intermediary to a final agreement. Only after this could the burying proceed after the branch was removed.

Like this one, sometimes we stumbled over new cultural situations. When we did, we asked later what was going on. Csaba found out that the young man who threw the branch was from an allied ethnic group and had a gripe against either the deceased or his family. The alliances between ethnic groups are very strong and there are certain rules that both must respect. What clued Csaba into the fact that something different was going on was that this young man wasn't a Bakwé and the old man of the village came to him on bended knee in humbleness. An old man never does that except to one from an allied group. By throwing down the branch on the coffin, the man was stopping the funeral. The deceased couldn't be buried until the young man was heard and appeased. This could only be done by the Patriarch who represented the village. So in the end, this one was resolved after they brought chickens, alcohol, and other items to the young man to satisfy him about the grievance that he had brought up.

Living in a village is intriguing because you keep learning new things that sometimes come in very unexpected ways. We were not the only ones learning either, as Janvier, from a northern group, had a lot to learn about Bakwé society as well.

What is fear? If you are a man, it is being chased by a mob of half-naked, hysterical women with pounding sticks in their hands. Janvier found that out once when he was in the wrong place at the wrong time. In Bakwé society, if a woman died in childbirth, all Bakwé women will go on a ritual rampage by stripping off their excess clothing (a sign of true rage), taking their pestles and storming around the village yelling in anger at all men for being the root cause of this death. The men hide in their houses while this is taking place, or they could get beaten by the mob.

Janvier, not being Bakwé, had the misfortune of entering the village during one of these sensitive moments. He heard yelling and turned around to see fifty enraged, half-naked women rushing at him with their pestles. He took off at a run and dove into his house shutting the door behind him. The mob then turned away to look for other hapless males. Janvier learned that the better part of valor when you don't know what to do in a new situation is to just run for cover.

It saddened us every time we heard of a death or went to a funeral because we knew that it was too late for these people to decide on following the Lord. Yet, we had to give that aspect over to the Lord who kept all things in His hands, and we needed to continue to concentrate on the living. This aspect was brought to the forefront of our minds one day when we went to greet those at the funeral of an old woman who had just died.

At the courtyard, we greeted the elders who were sitting in a circle by the house. They showed us seats and we sat down. The news was given to us by one of the elders about the day's events leading up to the old woman's death. As the conversation went back and forth in their soft, tonal language, Csaba looked around at all these men with a deeper thoughtfulness, and saw old Siwi the Harrist priest, a joker who always made people laugh. Then there was Alexis's father who always wore the traditional African cloth wrapped around him, and Csaba remembered that he had almost died of pneumonia last year. There was the chief, Yahou, who was one of the first to greet Csaba in the village, and Lucien who insisted that we pronounced Bakwé flawlessly, and old man Basa with his wrinkled face and work-roughened hands. These were all people we knew. They had their stories and lives in this little village. And this village was connected with the whole of Bakwé land that had been without the saving knowledge of Jesus Christ for as long as anyone could remember.

Csaba looked at them and knew how quickly the cycle of life turned, and he wondered when the time for these men would run out. Many had been told the gospel, but they still remained hardened. He longed to get the scriptures into their hands to speak to them in their own language, in a way that French never could. He longed for the day when the region would turn to Christ. But the team was still in the process of getting the Bible translated, and that would still take some time yet.

So, in the meantime, Csaba and his team worked hard on finding the right

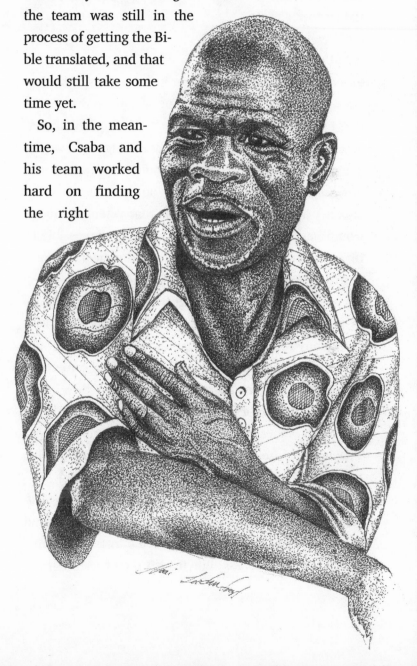

Bakwé words for certain key Biblical terms. It was like going on a treasure hunt with words, and as we saw earlier, some of the terms were really hard to find, like the word for grace.

GRACE

When looking for an equivalent in Bakwé for *grace,* Csaba had to first study the meaning of the word in Greek and the context in which it was used. English translations translate the Greek word *charis* using these words: *grace, favor, pleasure, thanks, liberality, credit, good-will, benefit, gift,* or *honor,* depending on the context. What makes translation complicated is that when you move from one language to another it is often impossible to find one word that can translate all the meanings of a particular word like *charis* into all the contexts.

For example, finding the right word to translate *grace* in the particular context of *unmerited favor* in Bakwé took many months. The Bakwé didn't have a word that meant *unmerited favor.* So, they tried to find something that was as close as possible. They first tried to incorporate the word for *liver,* because the Bakwé used it in the word for *mercy* which was literally *compassion-liver.* This was a close concept and related to grace, but this term wasn't quite adequate, so they kept looking.

'Nanaplɛ was tried next, which literally meant *good-good liver* or *niceness of God.* But it was too common and not as strong as it needed to be. Then they tried *'Nanakʋ* which meant *goodness.* But it also didn't seem strong

enough. They needed that particular word for other things when God's goodness was talked about. Finally, they settled on *-Gbinanakʋ,* which, if translated literally, meant *bountifulness,* and that fit the best. There would be a rounding out of the full meaning of this word over time as the scriptures were taught and used.

WORSHIP

Early on in the translation they were looking for a good word for *worship.* The word that was most natural and clear was *-pʋpʋ*a which meant *to adore, to worship.* But the Bakwé Christians resisted using this word because of its use in their traditional religion. So they settled for the word *bibie* which meant *to pray.* This word had an extended meaning that could possibly work, but over time they kept coming back to *-pʋpʋa.* Finally, near the end of the translation of the New Testament they had a big discussion and the Bakwé Christians agreed that rather than use *bibie,* it was best to redeem the word *-pʋpʋa* from its negative context. After all, it was the best word to use, and in time the practice of venerating the ancestors and idols would fade away as the church grew.

Even though Csaba was making great advances on the translation side of things, over in my domain back at the house, things kept falling apart.

CHAPTER TWENTY-TWO

VACATION

I wrote an email to a friend in the States:

> Well, we are plunged into darkness again. Our generator broke down and it will take more to fix it than we thought. We are now back to huddling around the kerosene lanterns at night because the generator charged the batteries that ran our 12-volt lights.
>
> These fun memories around the kerosene lantern will be added to the memories we had of tramping out to the latrine at night with a kerosene lantern when the indoor toilet quit working. The bright

side is that the indoor toilets are now working! What is a lack of lights compared to that?

The biggest effect of not having a generator is that the computer work for the office has had to wait for adequate sun for the solar panels to operate. Yesterday the team was just sitting around doing nothing since their computers weren't getting enough juice to run on. To try to get around this problem, Csaba ran the truck in the morning for several hours so that its energy could be channeled to the inverter for the computers.

In the meantime, I had to go down to the office during work hours to type out my emails. This was not exactly pleasant because the office was a place where four sweaty men were cramped in a relatively small mud and stick room with no fans, in a very humid climate. Since I am the public relations communicator for the ministry, I must put up with these little inconveniences.

It seems like a lot of things are breaking down on us lately, but this is nothing unusual for the time that we've been here.

I'm going to sign off now to get some much-needed fresh air.

Love,

Lisa

PS. Oh, we had a driver ant invasion last night near the chicken pen. Armed with cans of bug-spray,

we were able to break their ranks and divert them
away from the chicken pen. But then they headed
up toward the house!!

With things constantly breaking down or lacking altogether, along with the heat and humidity that con-
tinuously sapped our energy, we were very grateful
that God had provided the ocean less than a two hour's
drive away.

⚜

After arriving in San Pedro, we headed to the beach
and set down our things. Above us the coconut trees
sounded like giant rattles that brushed the sky, as they
swayed gently in the steady ocean breeze. Beyond us,
the ocean was wild with movement, and each swell
that rose and fell, danced with the sun's light in contin-
uously shifting patterns. As the
swells neared shore, their
tops broke free, spill-
ing their boun-
ty of lighted,
frothy foam
down

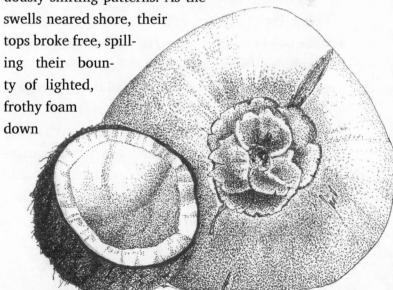

their steep walls. This bubbling mass raced towards shore in wild abandon pushed by the force of the wave. When the beach and the water collided, the waves cast their burden of light for a final time, throwing a thousand sparkling diamonds onto the shore. Some of these diamonds were swept back out to sea to return to their origin, while others slowly sank in little bubbles in the sand.

Since the conditions were just right for body surfing, we quickly waded into the warm, aquamarine ocean with our body surfing boards in hand. The strength of the waves made walking difficult, but we pushed past this tumult to the spot just before the big swells broke. Once in our positions, we stood our ground with the foaming, writhing water all around us. The kids and I faced the oncoming waves waiting for just the right one. Hans and Andreas were beside me with their boards, fighting to keep from being knocked off guard by the constant pulling of the water.

I tensed with excitement as I saw a big one coming, just the one I wanted. I waited till the crest of the wave almost hit me before I pushed off. Both Hans and Andreas pushed off too and we were all riding the wave with its mighty force driving us towards shore.

As we were sweeping into a rapidly approaching beach, a cross-wave hit our boards with a smack, causing a sharp lift and drop, then a resurgent rise. The white water churned around our faces, spitting foam that obscured our view. I managed to stay on my board and noticed that Hans and Andreas, just down the wave from me, were hanging on still. Once past this turbulence, the white water receded again, and we were plunged back into the glory of the dancing sunlight and the approaching beach as we rode our violently breaking horses beneath us. I looked over to my side and saw the boys' heads bathed in foamy light crested all around by the ever-curling wave.

Hans looked over at me and smiled through the spray. I thought to myself, "My, how God has blessed us, over and over again." In another instant, we were all hurled onto the sand and ground into it as the wave swept up and around us. Having deposited its burden on the shore, it returned back once more to the sea.

CHAPTER TWENTY-THREE

WHEN WE WERE YOUNG

Our children are an important part of our lives. We wanted to make sure we spent unrushed time with them and that life wasn't all work. Missionaries can be such workaholics that the children can get pushed to the side. With everything crying out with its urgency, the little things that make up for raising a child which add up over time can get left out. But even if missionaries classically operate in the crisis mode, that is not a sustainable pace for the long term without something giving, and that something should never be our children.

Raising children well to follow the Lord is more important than all the mission work in the world, because these children are given to us directly by God to raise and not to another. They are our first mission field and priority. If we can't do this well, how can we do the other? God will give the grace and time needed as parents look to Him because He is always faithful to give what we need for what He asks us to do.

We had to be diligent to make sure the needs of our children were met, both physically and emotionally. This was not easy in a village that seemed to always need us—constantly. But through God's mercy and grace, we made it work, and the children grew up to love the Lord and follow in His paths. And by His grace, we were also able to complete our work on the New Testament, even though it would prove to be very difficult at times. Here are some glimpses into those younger years and some of the seemingly insignificant things that helped make their childhood fun.

A DATE WITH DADDY IN ABIDJAN

Noai walked into the café with her hand held tightly in her daddy's hand. This five-year-old little girl was sheer excitement and anticipation as they were seated at a table in the middle of a crowded room. There were Europeans and Africans alike all enjoying the morning over a cup of coffee and croissant in this hotel-café in Abidjan. Yet, Csaba did not order a croissant but ice cream for his eager young daughter. She was on a date with her daddy and only the best would do.

After the order was put in and a cup of coffee brought for Csaba, Noai surveyed the table and discovered a bowl of sugar lumps just doing nothing in the middle of the table. So, she put a lump to use by dipping it in Csaba's coffee. She swirled it around before biting off one end, savoring it. When the last coffee-flavored bite disappeared into her mouth, she went for another lump with another dip into the steaming cup, all the while chatting happily to her father.

The waiter brought out her chocolate ice cream with a cookie stuck in one side. Noai's eyes grew big as the ice cream was placed in front of her. Ice cream was a rare treat that we only experienced twice a year when we came into the city from the village. She looked up at her father and smiled with appreciation for this wonderful thing that was just set before her. She looked at the smooth sides of the ice cream and the arrangement of the glassy, chocolate balls. This texture wanted touching, so she took her finger and ran it along the side of the ball experiencing its coldness, until her finger swiped into the creamy base and came back with a cold lump that made its way into her mouth. It also made its way down her arm as well. Csaba glanced around the room to see who might be watching, and gently suggested that Noai use her spoon because over at the next table, a man was staring at them.

Noai procured her spoon and started eating away, chatting about everything in general but nothing in particular while Csaba sipped on his coffee and made favorable interjections at appropriate times. As she enjoyed, Csaba noticed that some of the ice cream had

slid to the corners of her mouth and onto her cheeks.
Again, there was that man looking their way. Csaba
quickly handed her something to wipe her mouth with
yet hesitated to say anything negative to his daughter since she was enjoying herself so. Some of the ice
cream even ended up all the way down her shirt when
she accidentally dropped her spoon. Quick as a flash,
Noai dove under the table in a bouncy effort to rescue
her utensil from its fate on the floor. She brought the
spoon back up where Csaba wiped it off and the little
connoisseur "went to" again. Looking at the mess on
the table, Csaba wondered if his wee date was out of
place in so posh an establishment.

When the last of the ice cream was gone and the remaining bit of cookie eaten, Noai stole her fingers to the
sugar bowl for one final lump that would be dipped in
the almost diminished coffee. With that ritual done, she
gave Csaba a big chocolate hug and said with appreciation, "Thank you Daddy," then bounced off to look at
the displays in the window while he paid the waiter.

As Csaba got up from the table, he noticed hesitat-
ingly that the man who had been staring at them the
whole time was now coming towards him to talk. The
man approached and said, "Hello. I'm a businessman
who travels a lot. I've been watching you and your
daughter. She acts just like my five-year-old daughter
at home." He smiled, then shook his head in a far off,
sad way and continued, "I've been gone too long from
her. What you have is precious. Hang onto it."

"Thank you, sir, I will," was Csaba's reply. Then Csaba went to find his bouncy, chocolate-dotted daughter and gave her one last hug before the duo went back to the truck.

WILD BOAR HUNTING

The kids brought us much joy and hilarity with their funny antics. We were so thankful that we had the privilege of being a part of their lives and watching them grow.

One night, Csaba was out in the forest with some friends trying to get a wild beehive from a fallen tree. As they walked, the men felt that something was following them because they had heard grunts in the dark depths behind them. Since wild boar can be nasty, they made haste to move on. It was an exciting time, and Csaba had it in the back of his mind that one day he would actually go out and hunt that boar with his shot gun. But time in a busy translation schedule had never seemed to allow it, yet that wild boar episode provided a fascinating story for our young children. The one who seemed to be the most enthralled was our three-year-old son, Andreas. There he sat with his blue eyes as big as saucers riveted on daddy, who recounted the episode in all its captivating detail over and over. Andreas would soak up every word with the sheer excitement and horror of it all. Wild boars, imagine!

I'm sure in his young mind he was wanting to rid the world of dangerous animals. So one day I saw my courageous little boy put on his rain boots and grab his trusty, cassava-stick gun. He then penetrated the wilds of our backyard, even going up to a stone's throw away from the house all by himself, to hunt that elusive wild boar. I saw him stalking around corners and peering into the shadows of flower bushes. This seemed to occupy much of his time that afternoon. I went out there and asked him how things were going. He looked at me in his deadly-serious way and said in his own words that he hadn't been able to find any wild boar yet, but not to worry, he would shoot dead any that came onto the premises. I told him how relieved I was to hear that.

Day after day would find Andreas out with his cassava stick gun waiting for wild boars. He had dubbed himself Lord Protector of the yard. Hans, seeing that Andreas's attempts always met with naught, had wanted to give him something real to shoot at with his stick, so one day he slipped out of the house and into the backyard undetected. Once he was situated quite hidden in a flower bush, he started to make wild boar sounds. Hans watched from the bushes to see what would happen. He saw Andreas's blue eyes widening to their utter limits, then Andreas's little legs pumping their way up to the house as fast as they would go.

Hans laughed. Poor Andreas! He hadn't banked on there being real wild boar out in our backyard, even if it was the Hans type. The old cassava stick gun would sit on the shelf, and hunting would cease for a while until the lure of it would bring Andreas back much later. But next time he would be making real bamboo bows and arrows along with spring traps to attempt catching the wildlife on our property.

THE TEA PARTY

Noai, seven years old, had a prized china tea set sent from Grandma for Christmas. China tea sets were meant to be used, but the only problem she faced was the limited guest possibilities, especially when I was busy with the housework. During one of these times, she decided to enlist her brothers to fill the guest list. This seemed to be a wonderful solution to her problem until she found out that her brothers' idea of tea parties was to eat the cookies and run with no decent conversation in polite society to be had. Since this lack of etiquette could not be overcome, Noai soon found other options. And I have to admit, the guests she invited were certainly of a peculiar kind. They had unusual tastes, unusual ways of drinking tea, unusual manners and were all of a rather small size. Her first guests had beaks for eating, fluff for outfits, and were the proud offspring of our mama hen; yes, they would do nicely.

Much fuss was put into the preparations for the tea party. Seeds were smashed and pounded into seed cakes which were artfully arranged on the plates with millet and corn used as a border to adorn the side. It had that artist's touch. The water was poured into the cups and the party hats were lovingly made, decorated, and set by each plate. Then she set out to catch her guests. The boys were also taking an interest when they saw the guest list, and they rushed out to help capture them.

Once procured, the guests were placed by their plates to get their party hats on, but instead of calmly waiting for their party-finery, they immediately set to devouring the seed cakes. Noai rebuked them for their rudeness and scooped them up in her arms. The guests were terribly indignant about being interrupted from their meal and complained in a most unbecoming manner down in the folds of her skirt. One by one Noai picked up a chick and put its little party hat on with the rubber band underneath. Then she set down the chick in her lap and picked up the next one. When all their hats were on, she put them down by their plates. Yet, for all her efforts, half the chicks' hats slid under their fuzzy little necks like some sort of grotesque tie. This did not bother the participants much as they took to attacking their plates once again, gobbling grain with their pointed ties bobbing in the way.

Noai was amazed; the guests hardly came up for air. They also knocked over the teacups without an apology and stood on their plates while they ate. They greedily dove for their neighbor's food and basically acted in a very heathen manner. Noai rebuked them all for their lack of etiquette but they paid her no mind. Once the food was gone, they fidgeted and complained. She scooped them up again in her lap, disentangled the guests from their party hats, then took them back to their mama. Was the party a success? It certainly was to Noai who couldn't help but giggle at their funny antics. To have a party with live guests was far more interesting than all the inanimate dolls in the world, even if these guests did need a lesson on manners.

Over the course of years while we lived in the village, Noai invited many guests to her tea parties. Along with her chickens, she invited our mama cat who was put in a dress bearing the look of cat martyrdom, a rabbit that ended up being quite the bore until the dog arrived and made her scream, and a deviant mongoose who was a bit of a wild card. It was the mongoose that needed the most instruction on manners because she had none. She kept slipping out of her dress and growling at anyone who came near her plate. She gobbled up her food in an atrocious manner and then kept leaving the party to explore the house, which endangered our furniture to her way of marking territory. But, in my opinion, she was the funniest

guest of all, because she looked the most hilarious in a dress.

Yes, the old china tea set got a lot of use.

YE OLDE FISHING EXPEDITION

Andreas had a fascination with fishing and catching things. His training started when he was quite young. He was always the instigator of the fishing projects and recruited my assistance, whether it was helping him rig up a bamboo pole for our pond, or later enlisting me to untangle the interminable mess of our old casting lines. But let me take you way back to the beginning of his fishing career to a living room that somehow had turned into an ocean.

It was another wonderful day to be alive if you were three, and today's project had to do with fishing. Andreas wanted me to make him a fishing pole, so I constructed one out of a curtain rod. He was thrilled because it was no ordinary fishing rod—it was adjustable! One could make it go in and out at will. It even had a line made of tape (no string to be had at the time) and a cardboard hook. He was excited about it, but something was missing. Why of course! The expedition was incomplete without all the necessary equipment, so he enlisted me to make a cardboard tackle box. Every fisherman needed a tackle box! We set about the task and soon made compartments for all the fish he would catch plus space for his cardboard worms and tackle.

Now he could begin. But wait, something else was missing. How can one be a true fisherman without fish? This too had to be remedied, and Noai and I were enlisted to make a whole ocean full of fish, big ones and little ones of all the colors of the rainbow. To top that off, we even drew silly expressions on their faces to make them look more authentic. Now his fishing expedition was complete. Andreas again was thrilled in a way that only a three-year-old fishing enthusiast can be.

He climbed up on his cushioned yacht and dipped his line in the vast ocean of our living room. He looked down anxiously, waiting for the next stage to happen which was slowly unfolding on the ocean floor as Noai magically brought these cardboard fishes to life.

Noai grabbed a fish, put it on the hook then gave a sharp tug. Andreas yelled that he had got a big one and up it went into his yacht on the couch. It was admired by all, then taken off the hook and put into the tackle box. Down again went the cardboard hook and worm to seek new quarry under the sea, and again came the expected tug and subsequent fish. But as every fisherman knows, fish can be unpredictable, and that day proved no exception.

Andreas found that sometimes the worms were stolen off his hook and no fish were to be had. This upset the fisherman to a righteous fury, and he looked straight into the deep blue waters and yelled to Neptuness to get on with it. Neptuness responded back with,

"But you can't have the little ones since they're still babies. Here, take this big, fat daddy one."

And up again would go another fish into the happy fisherman's lap. Then a terrible thing happened to the fishing expedition. Jeremiah, the abominable sea monster, woke up from his slumber and toddled off with the excess fishes in his chubby little arms. Neptuness had to fetch them back, which caused the sea monster to howl. Since the sea monster had to be appeased, fishing stopped for the day.

In the process of the daily ups and downs, hardships and joys of raising children, we always had to keep our eyes on the Lord and the grander scheme of things. Many years from now when those in our work will have long forgotten us, our children will remember, and will either be grateful for the love and care given them or will resent having been neglected as taking second place to the work.

CHAPTER TWENTY-FOUR

TRANSLATION CHECKS

Translation checks are an important part of the process to make sure that the team has translated a book correctly. After Csaba and his Bakwé colleagues finish translating a book and before they go to the city to meet with a consultant, they get a written back translation of the text done. This is where a Bakwé person who has never been a part of the translation process reads the Bakwé text and writes it into a very literal French, word for word. This document is then sent to the consultant in the city prior to the team meeting with them in person.

In preparation to the team coming, the consultant, who doesn't know the language, reads the back translation and prepares questions that he wants to ask the team about the text. When the team sits down in person with the consultant, each verse of the Bakwé text is read out loud by one of the Bakwé men, usually Alexis. Then another Bakwé will do an oral translation of that portion into French, which the consultant is fluent in. The consultant will then check his notes from the text that was sent him earlier against the oral translation to see if there are any problems to be addressed. He will be looking for where the French differs too much from the original Greek. This clues him in to whether a wrong Bakwé word has been used or a concept hasn't carried across successfully from one language to the other.

Here is a peek into the consultant check on Hebrews 8:5:

The verse was first read out loud: "who serve the copy and shadow of the heavenly things, as Moses was divinely instructed when he was about to make the tabernacle."

After this reading, an oral translation into French was given for the consultant. The consultant then noticed that both the written and oral back translations used the French word *tente* for tabernacle, so the consultant asked them, "Explain to me what kind of shelter or tent does this Bakwé word have in the place of tabernacle? Is it a permanent structure or temporary? What is it made of?"

The team explained that the word meant a shelter usually made of palm branches. The consultant recounted how the Jews made their tabernacle out of animal skins. He asked them what other types of temporary structures the Bakwé had that could be used in place of this word. When the team could not find any other word except the one they had already chosen, they agreed to change it to the phrase *animal skin tent.*

Consultants are invaluable to us because their job is to make sure the team is being faithful to the Greek and clear in their translation down to the detail. The consultants also bring their experience from working with related languages to the session as well. Csaba and the team always came away from a consultant check exhausted but encouraged that they had a better translation than before. Once the consultant signed off on a book, then they were free to publish trial copies. These sessions were for the book by book checks, but before the final publication of the New Testament could be done, there were a number of other checks as well.

FINAL CHECKS

Consistency check: This check looks at the consistency of our use of biblical key terms, key theological concepts, names of places and people, and parallel passages both in the Gospels and throughout the entire translation. This check makes sure that the translation is consistent in using the same Bakwé words for concepts in all the passages. It also checks to see if the spelling is consistent for all the names.

Format and style check: This check looks at punctuation, chapter and verse numbers, titles, maps, pictures, glossary, and footnotes.

Proofreading check: The translation is printed and proofread from top to bottom by various readers. Even before this consultant check, it is read over multiple times.

Oral read-through check: The entire translation is read out loud in the presence of selected native Bakwé speakers, chosen from different churches across the region. At this point, the goal is to try and catch anything that sounds wrong in the flow or is missing to round out a concept.

Typesetting: This is done by a trained typesetter who imports the text into a professional publishing software program. The typesetter formats each page, making adjustments to the pages, illustrations, footnotes, etc. Then the translators read every page again to make sure there are no errors, such as words hyphenated wrongly.

Final publication: After several more read-throughs by the team of the entire New Testament, the manuscript is sent to Dallas Scripture Publishing center and the last formatting checks are run there. If there are no changes, then the manuscript is cleared to be printed in South Korea.

Printing: After it is printed in South Korea, then it is shipped by boat back to Africa. After that, a dedication takes place and the Bible is put into the hands of the people.

There was so much yet to do for us to get to that point, and it all took time. We were still in the middle of the translation when we started feeling the tensions of a growing political unrest. It was brewing like a simmering cauldron underneath. We didn't know when or if it would blow, but the weight of that situation was always present while in Africa. We hoped and prayed that the political situation would simmer down. In the meantime, we were relieved to go back to the US for a year of furlough where there was no looming political tension.

CHAPTER TWENTY-FIVE

FURLOUGH

While on furlough in Idaho, we enrolled the kids in the Christian school where they were reunited with their friends. We also spoke to groups, visited some supporting churches, and then settled down as Csaba took care of all that needed to be done before our return to the field which, unknown to us at the time, was not to take place as we had planned. Yet we were thankful that we had come home when we did because I had become increasingly exhausted from a low-lying chronic fatigue while in the village.

Furloughs were usually a time for us to regain our strength and get in a little rest and relaxation before we went back. Usually by the end of a term on the mission field, we were pretty exhausted both physically and emotionally. But back in the States we could regain strength since we didn't have to deal with the constant travel, the endless problems and crises in the village, the heat, the sickness, and periodic deaths that were just a part of life there. We were also free from concern about the robbers and gangs that were prevalent in troubled times. Furlough was definitely needed after each term, and we were thankful that our home church had provided enough support for us that we didn't have to travel around to raise it. We could go back refreshed to face all the problems that would naturally come our way by being on the mission field.

Part of recharging for me was enjoying God's big beautiful world in the nature around us. Especially after a long winter.

It was one of those magical days in spring. The weather turned unexpectedly warm, the sun peeked out from behind those clouds, and the spring air was so enticing that Noai and I decided to take a walk on the hill behind our house in Moscow, Idaho. Since we lived for most of the time in the tropics, we were not used to the winter, or the somberness of a sunless period, or the coldness that forced us to stay indoors for long stretches of time.

So, we walked up the giant hill, tender with fresh growth from the spring rains and bathed in the afternoon sun. I was ambling slowly, and Noai slower still, since she had seen a patch of wildflowers that wanted picking. After gathering these, she bent down to pick a dandelion, then blew its little tuft of parachuted men into the wind to take their journey to fields beyond.

We walked on, entering a lush place where the grass's purple heads bobbed in the wind, causing a rippling effect in a sea of lavender. It was there that gravity and the drunkenness of a warm sunny day after a long winter hit us. We lay down in that patch, burying ourselves from view, entering into another miniature world. With our faces low to the ground, in the midst of this grassy kingdom, we could see chambers and corridors with earthen floors and green walls, damp and sweet, where field mice played. The sun was warm and our grassy bed intoxicating with its sweet smell filling the air, so we turned over and sucked on the ends of grass stalks and lay there as if time had no meaning. We lay there for a while—almost an eternity, until the giant hill beckoned, and we moved on.

As we walked up that hill nearing the top, all that we could see was sky and hill above us. Nothing else existed until we reached the top where a new world came into view. The low mountains of Moscow lazily graced the skyline with their dark fir forests alternately bathed in patches of light or shadow depending on the clouds bobbing over them. We stopped to drink it in, the town, the mountains and the land as it stretched away, washed in a hazy light that spread into a bluish beyond.

As I looked at all this beauty before me, I wondered how many other folks that day would be out in the countryside taking delight in this lazy spring day. Some people would say that missionaries live in want with few luxuries to enjoy, but to us, all that God gives is a king's feast.

While on furloughs we enjoyed camping as a family.

After a long drive, we arrived at a campground in the mountains of the Saw Tooth National Forest. Fishing was something the kids looked forward to while camping, since mountains and trout were scarce in our corner of Ivory Coast. So I took the kids fishing in a mountain stream while Csaba cooked dinner back at camp.

I sat there on the bridge looking down at the brook that churned underneath me. I followed its course until my eye caught a fishing line jerking with the current. At the other end Jeremiah held the stick attached to the line, fixing his gaze intently at the rushing surface. He studied that line, bobbing with the weight of the current. I then looked over and saw Noai. She also had a stick in her hand with a makeshift line attached to it too, but somehow between the bridge and the stream bank, she had managed to eliminate any hopes of fishing for

that day. She spent her time sitting on the rocks patient-
ly trying to untangle her line. When this interminable
mess became too time consuming, she put down the tangle and sat there dreamily watching the water flowing
over the rocks. Then something caught her eye—a duckling. She rose from her rock and slipped into the water
towards the unsuspecting creature.

Meanwhile, on the bridge, Jeremiah saw a silver flash
and the bait was gone. He pulled on his line and excitedly yelled, "I got a fish!" then accidentally dropped the
line on the wooden bridge with a thunk. I was able to
stop it before it went over the edge, and soon a small
trout was pulled in. The trout was put in our laundry
bag and tied to a stick by the rushing river where Hans
was building some dams out of rocks. In fact, a whole
reconstruction of that side of the stream bank was un-
derway with the master builder busy at work.

Andreas was on the opposite side of the stream fishing, but I could tell he wasn't satisfied with his position
since he kept changing it constantly. After Jeremiah
pulled in his fish, he decided that the bridge was now
a great spot to fish too. Noai, down below, had gotten
pretty wet tracking her elusive duckling. Half of her
was now soaked, while the other half was peppered
with small bits of broken-off branches and leaves. Yet
that duckling kept giving her the slip.

Since Csaba would soon have dinner ready, we decided it was time to go back to camp and cook Jeremiah's trout. The chilly evening was still to come with

a campfire that would roast the front half of us while leaving the back half pretty cold, and with marshmallows that would light up like fireworks then die down again to a burnt remnant with a squishy middle. There would be the sleeping bags on hard ground that somehow still felt cozy as one listened to the night noises in the fir trees overhead. Yes, camping was fun.

FAMILY REUNION IN MICHIGAN

We had other experiences of camping while on furlough as well, which were more like the *Fine and Pleasant Misery*[3] type.

We had arrived at a campground in Michigan for a family reunion. It was dark and I could hear the steady rain falling on our tent. I lay in my sleeping bag thankful that we were warm and dry inside, or were we? I felt the tent fabric under my sleeping bag—wet. I moved my sleeping bag over to get out of the puddle and found that the puddle had followed me. I muttered under my breath about rain and tents when Noai gleefully sat up on her camping pad and said, "Oh neat! I'm floating!"

I was glad she had such a positive outlook on life and its little pleasures. Anyhow, I scrunched up my sleeping bag close to Csaba's on a semi-dry spot and

3 The title of a 1968 book by Patrick McManus.

tried to go back to sleep. Noai continued to revel in her boat and drifted off to sleep on the high seas. It rained most of the night and there were puddles everywhere. In fact, our tent was sitting in one. Csaba called it a character-building experience. I called it a mess.

We had finally arrived in Michigan to camp with my sister, brother and their families along with my parents for our reunion and we were going to enjoy it! The next day, bright and early, my kids wanted to go fishing to try out their bass lures that they had found in the weeds by the lake. But, what with the water level being under two feet at the shoreline and not having a suitable casting rod to our name, we decided to go and buy two dollars' worth of worms at the camp store to aid the fishermen. We just needed to wait until dawn to go out and catch all those fish.

I got up early and woke Noai and Jeremiah, whose sleeping pads were still wet from the night's rains. The next trick was to get at Andreas over in my brother Dave's dry tent. Andreas had slept over there with Hans due to the lake in ours. Getting Andreas out without waking Dave up would be a bit of a trick. My brother had made it pretty clear that he didn't want to be wakened before seven a.m.—come fishing or high waters. It was six a.m., and the time was getting away, so I unzipped the screening and found Andreas's feet. I nudged him—no response. I then tried to pinch his toes, but he was out cold. Since Andreas's sleeping bag was right by the door, I pulled him out very slowly while he slept. He woke up confused when he hit the ground outside the tent but soon came to his senses. I was happy that I had succeeded at least, in not waking my brother. But it turned out that I needn't have been so careful because we then went through our forgetting-things-in-the-car routine. Csaba wanted me always to shut the doors after opening them and I dutifully obeyed. We were so good at forgetting things that Dave woke up and gave me one of his exasperated-brother looks at six fifteen a.m.—sigh. Csaba was still asleep.

After all that noise, little Stevie (two years old), got up and watched us fish. The fish were really biting that morning and a nice blue gill was soon caught. Stevie got so excited by the fish that, to christen the event, he threw a large stone in the water to help us out. Since now our spot was fish-less, we decided to move to another site, ten feet away. While there, the boys caught three other small fish. We filled a bucket and dumped them in. With all the trouble that it took to catch the fish, we wanted to experience them a little in our tiny bucket lake before we released them.

Stevie was fascinated by these fish and climbed onto a chair to watch them. When he went to get off the chair, he fell into our bucket, rear-end style, with the terrified fish underneath. This was more than the fish or Stevie had bargained for. I helped a confused, wet boy out of our bucket lake. After keeping the larger blue gill, I helped the three confused, smaller fish back to the real lake where they disappeared into its murky depths.

In memory of those expensive worms, we ate our two-dollar blue gill for supper, and everyone took a tiny bite. And of course, that night it still rained, and we still floated, but at least we were together as an extended family again after the long years of separation. It would take more than rain to cause us to regret our camping trip, because the hardest aspect of being on the mission field (separation) was being eased, if only for a moment, on this rain-soaked site in Michigan.

CHAPTER TWENTY-SIX

TRIALS

We flew back to Ivory Coast refreshed but found that the problems in the country hadn't abated but grown in our absence, which was not very encouraging. We wondered what was happening to this country, because Ivory Coast had been one of the most stable and prosperous of all the West African nations for so long. But this had only lasted until the old president had died. With his successor Henri Konan Bedié came some strife at a low level. Over the years, the strife grew until finally there was a successful coup with the General Robert Guéï taking over the presidency from the ousted President Bedié in December of 1999. He said he was going to hold elections in a year, and he was good to his word.

We had flown into the country after furlough about four months before the elections, which turned out to be a mistake. We were met at the airport by one of our colleagues who said, "Everyone else is leaving because they are afraid of potential unrest at the coming elections. It is a welcome sight to see someone actually arriving."

This was not very reassuring. After we settled in the village, we heard news of demonstrations and pockets of rioting that erupted here and there as the tensions grew. Then the presidential elections were held with General Guéï and Laurent Gbagbo as the main contenders. The results were supposed to come out in a couple days. But something happened in the meantime that would turn our world upside down.

We got up in the morning and turned on the radio to hear that there was heavy gun fighting in Abidjan. We listened in shocked silence. We remembered the unusual events of the previous day. As votes came in region by region, the radio gave a tally for the ongoing results. It had been a close race for most of it until one of the candidates appeared to be losing midway. This surprised us since the losing candidate was General Guéï who had gained power by the recent coup less than a year ago.

After the radio announced that Gbagbo was in the lead, the radio went dead and the world was cut off from us. We tried the phones, but they were dead as well. We heard from folks in town that said their TVs didn't work. There seemed to be no way to get information from the outside. What was going on? Then the General who had been losing got on the air and announced that the results were now all in, and that he had won. He supplied no evidence or proof.

That was all we knew until the next morning when the radio told of the events that had happened in Abidjan the night before. According to the reports, the supporters of Laurent Gbagbo got upset when General Guéï announced his presidency and took to the streets in a rage. Then the military came out and supposedly were only firing in the air, but soon after it was reported that they were shooting at each other as the military split their loyalty. It looked serious. Our workers came in at eight a.m. and were excitedly talking about the situation. They huddled next to the radio to hear any more news. Knowing the patterns of other West African nations, Csaba realized the dangerous predicament we were now in. We could easily be trapped in the village if a civil war were to erupt. Since phones were now working in town, Csaba wanted to write an email to the elders of our church and let them know of our precarious situation. Just as Csaba was about to go to town to do email, Janvier came back. He had been sent to the market but returned shortly after when he found out that there were angry crowds on the road. Our world around us was seething.

We could hear the noise and confusion in the distance. Alexis, who had gone to check out the situation, got word that they had burned part of the market and were burning other things as well. People were just furious at the change of events and were taking it out on whatever they could. He said the crowd was on the march, bent on destruction, and coming our way toward the village. We called the kids inside. On the radio we heard that demonstrations of protests were happening in major cities all over the nation. People were angry and destroying things. Some people were even killing in all the confusion.

Janvier's wife was worried, and she brought her baby over from their house to stay in our kitchen. Since there was no school, the kids decided to pass the time by playing the boardgame *Life* in the living room. Where was I? I was sick in bed. The day before, I had felt really tired, weak, and faint, and went to bed. I felt a type of tiredness that might be something serious. The next day it was not quite as bad. I didn't have any real symptoms to speak of, so we were wondering if it couldn't be a light relapse of typhoid or an atypical case of malaria. We didn't know, but something hadn't been right for a while and seemed to be getting worse. Since we now had a good clinic and doctor in San Pedro, Csaba tried to call, but the doctor had already fled to get away from the large crowds that had taken to the streets. Travel now was out of the question and getting any response was impossible. Come what may, we were stuck in the village. Csaba looked at me and said, "We're in the hands of God, don't worry." He was praying, and so was I.

We stopped to listen. The noise from the angry crowd was slowly diminishing. Thankfully we realized that they had turned around and were going elsewhere for their demonstrations. We were relieved by this and Janvier's wife went home with her baby.

With that immediate threat gone, we went back to listen to the radio, and found out that the military was still shooting at each other. It looked like there was a violent civil war brewing underneath. France got on the air and threatened that if the General didn't step down, they would come in with arms and force him to do it. Somewhere during this time the General got on the air and gave his inaugural address. When Csaba heard this, he was concerned and came into the room where I was lying and started to pack a bag with his important files. I asked him what he was doing, and he said, "The situation is intensifying somewhat, and just as a precaution I'm packing a few things. I don't think we'll have to flee yet, so don't worry." I groaned inwardly. I didn't want to leave. We had just settled down after furlough, and all the traveling tired me out tremendously.

Then on the radio we heard that the military had quit shooting at each other and was unified once more.

The General went into hiding. Laurent Gbagbo got on the radio and announced that calm was returning to the city. He would reinstate the electoral committee and then continue to tally up the votes that would be announced in a day. I heard a loud cheer coming from the village. I asked Csaba what had happened, and he said that it was all over for now. I couldn't believe it. It was like a thunderstorm had blown in, then rushed back out leaving the area calm like before.

I relaxed until my thoughts were interrupted by a loud scream coming from our yard. "Oh no," I thought, "What next?"

I saw Andreas come bounding towards the house yelling, "Noai, get them off! Quick!"

Evidently Andreas had sat in a pile of driver ants and was now dancing around as Noai tried to pick them off his legs. Yes, things were getting back to normal here too.

President Gbagbo won the elections and now that he was in power, everything should have been right, but it wasn't. It continued to be a time of a slowly building tension which manifested itself in different ways. In the days that followed we heard that there was another unsuccessful coup attempt, and due to the unstable atmosphere, more armed robberies were taking place. We heard that armed bandits would enter restaurants and make people lie down on the floor and then take their money. They would stop cars on the road and take the car, leaving the families on the roadside. If people resisted, they could be shot. Bandits even entered houses in the evenings to steal. All this happened to missionaries we knew, but thankfully no one was killed.

One thing we hadn't fully realized was that things were building and leading to a chronically dangerous situation. We were like frogs in warm water that was slowly heating up. But we carried on as usual, traveling to workshops at Bouaké or going to our administrative center in Abidjan. While there, I could see the strain and tiredness on other missionaries' faces, especially those who lived in some of the country's hottest spots, like Bouaké. Even though we were not living in one of those hot spots, we still had armed gangs on the roads in our area too, and we heard different reports of their raids. It was disconcerting to hear how these gangs attacked and what they did to the victims, and we learned when it was safe to travel and when not. Certain times of the night we could not even be on the roads in an emergency. We also kept a tight control on who came on our property.

In Bouaké, where our workshop center was, there were repeated raids at night that really unsettled the community. Some of the bandits were actually caught. In one case a bandit dropped his ID card on the floor when he robbed a place. After the bandit left, the victims of the robbery picked up the ID and took it to the authorities. While they were reporting the card, the bandit walked in to report his missing card. The victims asked the authorities to arrest the man, but they wouldn't, because evidently, he was their friend. So the victims went to the French consulate with their story who then pulled strings and the guy was arrested.

In another case, a bandit robbed a Frenchman and took his vehicle. In the stolen car was the Frenchman's cell phone. After the bandit fled the premises in the stolen car, the Frenchman called his own cell phone and the bandit surprisingly answered. The Frenchman told the bandit in no uncertain terms that he wanted his car back, and since it had official plates, it could be tracked. So, the bandit decided that having this particular car was not a good idea and he told the Frenchman where he could find it. All of these events over time produced an unsettledness, like an unseen weight.

CHAPTER TWENTY-SEVEN

ON SEPTEMBER 19, 2002 WAR BROKE
out in Ivory Coast after another attempted coup. The
coup was being conducted by disloyal Ivorian soldiers
along with mercenaries from surrounding African
countries. They had come with serious war artillery.
By this time, thankfully, we were back in the United
States for what was supposed to be a short stay to look
at colleges for Hans. Yet, our mini furlough would end
up turning into an extended stay when we couldn't get
back to Ivory Coast due to the unrest that continued
to escalate in our absence. Having to remain in the
States while our colleagues were in Ivory Coast was
such an odd feeling because while we were living in
peace, they were living in the throes of war.

NO ISOLATED EVENT

It soon became apparent that there was a whole movement to take over the country. Other northern towns succumbed as gangs sought to control the whole region, town by town. It was a shock to us, especially when it looked like there would be no easy solution. One of the African translators with our mission said, "My country! What is happening to my beautiful country?!"

Then came the news that the western town of Man, four hours north, had a massacre. As town after town in the north and west fell to the rebels, we felt that our world as we knew it was crumbling over there. With each fresh news we got of the war, it was like someone hit us in the stomach with the ache lasting for days. Because we were painfully aware that the rebels had a goal to take over our area too.

During the time when the rebels took control of Bouaké (where our workshop center was located along with the missionary boarding school), we later heard the stories that happened from missionaries who were trapped inside the city. I find it amazing what God will ask of His people when He sends them overseas to the mission field. As we heard varying stories, it encouraged us how God sustains His children, because when God puts them through hard times, He goes through it with them, providing His help and strength every step of the way.

Our mission had fifteen people inside our workshop center at the time when the fighting erupted. One of our members, Karen DeGraaf, was attending the workshop at the time, while her husband, David, and their three school aged children remained back in Abidjan. At the center during one of the sessions, the attendees heard nearby gunfire and wondered what was going on. They found out from the news that there had been an attempted coup, and violent battles were going on in Abidjan, Bouaké, and Korhogo. In Bouaké, where they were currently, the opposition fighters were advancing as the government troops fought back. Those in the workshop could hear the gunfire getting louder and louder when someone suggested that they hold their sessions in the dorm rooms on the side that faced the courtyard.

In the meantime, John and Merri Holmes with Baptist Mid-Missions were sitting down to eat in their home in the suburbs of Bouaké when they heard machine gun fire and cannons going off pretty close to their house. They grabbed their plates and ran to the inner hallway. As they finished their meal, they could hear the gun battle raging outside which continued on for another three hours. They even heard bullets hitting their tin roof! During this time, they lay on the floor in the hall, singing, quoting scripture, and praying hard. Thankfully they had their phones with them as well, so they made contact with the outside world and found out that they were in a war zone and that the Embassy wanted to get them all out as soon as possible!

Back at the dorms, Karen and the others were hoping it would blow over and that the government would squelch this uprising. During this time of waiting, they didn't dare venture outside the walled compound, but thankfully, there were a few employees who were able to bring them fruit and vegetables. When the fighting continued, they realized this could last for longer than expected and they hauled food and water up to the dorm rooms so they could do all their eating and preparing in a safer, more sheltered place. Karen's husband, David, was concerned for her, and kept in contact by phone.

Back over at the Holmes's place, there had been a battle in the field behind their house that had left an estimated one hundred dead bodies. Merri tried comforting her four children by saying, "I can't tell you if we will make it out of here alive. But if we die, we'll all go to heaven and be there together." Some African friends were able to bring them food and water as well. As they waited and wondered what would happen next, they received messages and calls from around the world assuring them that they were being prayed for! This was encouraging because they were longing for a good night's sleep with no guns going off.

At one point during their ordeal, they saw Africans running down the street. They asked one of them what was happening, and he said that there was a rumor of a big battle that was going to take place, and that they were to all get off the streets! So, the Holmes secured themselves in their house again and prepared for the worst as they waited. John wrote in an update sent back home: "We are emotionally weary but have hope that it will be over soon. As we ate lunch today, we talked about how thankful we are to have a Father in heaven who sees and cares about us, no matter which continent we're on. It's a very special thing to have the peace of God in times of crisis."

Over at the center, Karen and the others heard rumors from the outside that the government was going to attempt to retake Bouaké and that a violent confrontation would likely take place. Not knowing how bad it would be, the workshop attendees stayed down that day, but thankfully nothing of that magnitude ended up taking place.

In the meantime, a plan was being formed up high to get people out of the war zone. The American embassy worked with the French to arrange a cease-fire with the rebels so that they could evacuate their people. First, the boarding school, just out of town, would be evacuated under a French military escort and then it was planned for the troops to swing by to get the others in town. These others included the Holmes, as well as those at our workshop center.

Those in the center waited and hoped. In the meantime, they still heard gunfire and wondered when and how it would work to get them out. On Monday evening, they went out in the courtyard for a much-needed stroll but were suddenly surrounded by the sound of heavy artillery fire. When they saw bullets fly across the yard, one missionary yelled, "Take cover and get down!" So, they ran into the building and hunkered down in the hallway while the building shook with the noise of the gunfire. That battle lasted for two hours. In the meantime, they were receiving phone calls from people all over, which was such a comfort.

On Tuesday, there was another battle that lasted three hours with some bullets even hitting the building. During this time, they held hands and prayed, and this knit them together in a closer bond because of the danger. They didn't panic even though it was terrifying to hear the battle raging outside the walls. But after days of waiting, they finally got word that the military had already evacuated the boarding school kids by a back route, and that they were left behind and would just have to wait; this made them wonder if they were ever going to get out of there and what would happen next?

Back at the Holmes's place, the day before, a friend at the boarding school told them to get their bags packed, and that the military would swing by to pick them up as well after the school was evacuated. But the next day the Holmes watched with dismay on their TV that the French military had taken the kids by a back route. After this, the Holmes's friend called them on the phone and said, "John, I'm afraid they've left you."

John said, "Why haven't you gone with them?"

His friend said, "Some of us refused to leave until we saw that all the missionaries had gotten out safely."

Discouraging as it was to be left behind, God had not forgotten them, and a short time later everyone got word they would be evacuated now. They were told to drive their vehicles to the designated meeting place to wait for all to congregate. When the missionaries arrived, they saw each other, and there were cries of joy and hugs all around. Then as a group, they left, and traveled first to a large city in a safer zone to spend the night before traveling to Abidjan the next day.

When Karen drove into the parking lot of the center in Abidjan, she saw her young kids playing in the yard. They saw her and were delighted but were still unaware of the danger she had just been through. But not so with the other missionaries and Africans who came running out of the building to greet them. There were hugs and tears of gratitude as they welcomed them back with thanksgiving to God for His mighty deliverance. Then David, Karen's husband, came out, and with tears of relief in his eyes, he embraced her as if he would never let her go. He thanked God over and over again for His mercy in sparing her life.

She wrote,

> Looking back, I saw courage in the leadership who tirelessly worked to get us out. I saw courage in my husband who waited and prayed on the other end not knowing what the result would be and I saw courage in my colleagues and friends, who were with me in those awful yet amazing hours

when life was held in a balance. And finally, I saw courage in those on the other end, praying and waiting for our escape. It made me aware of what an amazing community we have here as missionaries, one that I will never take for granted. I also realized what an awesome God we serve, that no matter what happens, God is our life, our protection and that He will never leave us.

All these people looked to the Lord during their time of need and found Him faithful. And there was blessing when God pulled the Christian community together both on the field and at home to pray. Yes, there was so much to be grateful for.

CHAPTER TWENTY-EIGHT

NEWS OF WAR

While we were in Idaho, we got news of atrocities from the war and how tough it was for those Ivorians who were displaced and lacked the necessities of life. It was one thing to hear about these things in a newspaper about a country you have never visited. It was quite another when you knew the places and the people who were hit by the suffering. During this time missionaries tried to contact their African co-workers to send them money or get them out of the war zone. And in the west, where our village was located, the area was slowly being taken over by a third rebel group aided by Liberian mercenary fighters. Many villagers had to flee into the bush and live the best way they could. Homes were destroyed, people killed or maimed. In the meantime, President Gbagbo was trying to negotiate a peace treaty with the rebels.

As the war went on with the probability of it lasting a long time, the missionary community dispersed. Since we were from different places, it was like our large missionary family was scattering to the four winds. Once missionaries were back in their home countries, we started making contact with each other again. There was something comforting in this, because no one else really understood the pain. I mean, how can people who live in peace back home understand those who are dealing with the impacts of war? For us, it was such an odd feeling to be actually living ourselves in daily peace and safety in the States, when those we cared about, our African friends and colleagues back in the village, were still living in a world that was dangerous and falling apart.

Csaba was able to keep in contact with Alexis by cell phone and told me that the team hadn't been working much. It was a time of high stress, especially when they got rumors of the rebels coming to their area. When they heard these rumors, the villagers went into hiding until it was proven that the threats were unfounded. Then there were the refugees who poured into our area from other villages further west, telling how cruel the rebels could be in their pillaging, killing, and burning. This made people jumpy and fearful of what could be in store for them. But so far, our village had remained untouched.

REMINISCING

We sent periodic updates to our supporters like usual. Csaba often asked me to do the portion on our family since we liked to add them into it too. I never sent this following update because I kept getting sidetracked with other thoughts, missing the world that we had left behind. It remained in my computer until I began writing this book.

Dear Friends and Supporters,

Thank you for your prayers as we wait out the war. It has been tough, but we are doing well. We have a good life in the States, and we are extremely thankful that God has chosen us to be here where everything is stable and calm. Here is an update on the family.

The kids are doing well. Let me recount to you what they have been doing. Andreas is in cross-country and I love to watch him methodically race with quiet determination. But, as I watch him run, I can remember in the not too distant past, in another country, in another world, a sweaty boy running barefoot on the soft, hot earth, carrying an indignant cat for company with an exuberant dog running by his side. I can see him now with all the others doing laps in our rice field, in humidity that you can cut with a knife as the thick thunderheads loom in the distance warning of an approaching storm.

Noai is also enjoying herself on furlough. She is in an art class that gives her much joy and creative outlet. Aside from that, she has her entourage of animals to take care of, namely her birds and a gerbil. She calls to her finches and they respond back in their own language. As I watch her play with her pets, I fade away to another time when I can see a graceful girl with streaming blond hair dash out of the house and past the lime tree with seven frantic baby chicks trying desperately to keep up with the only mother they have ever known. I then watch her plop down in the soft grass and gather her chicks around her, to enjoy the morning.

Jeremiah is busy at play in general. He likes climbing and attacking Andreas with apples. But, I think back to a little boy with wheat blond hair hiding in the thick tangled underbrush, brush so thick that it looks like an impenetrable wall of green choked with vines. He is crouching low, waiting with his homemade bow and arrows, waiting for an unsuspecting brother or two to pass by.

While Hans is not in school, he is down in his bedroom working on his creations which consist of various planes and gadgets. He is ever inventing, ever creating to improve on his latest model. As I think of him, I remember another boy over to the side, by the pond, on the bare earth, hard at work fashioning kingdoms out of clay under the mango tree, civilizations that would rage at war with one another if he could only convince his brothers and sister to fight him under the hot African sun.

Csaba is getting ready to teach at New St. Andrews College on missions. He is spending quite a bit of time behind his desk working out his course. In another world I see a missionary translator, beaded with sweat in a mud house crammed with four other African men, all working hard behind computers. With the fans humming, the computer keys clicking, and the soft tonal language spoken in the background, they would find yet another word that could fit a difficult concept.

And what have I been doing? I have been writing a book about our lives overseas. And in that book, in that other world, a missionary wife is huddled over a computer writing just one more story of the day's events before the approaching tropical storm comes in. The wind is starting to blow, the sky is darkening, and she closes down the computer to dash out and retrieve the laundry before the storm envelopes their entire lives.

And like a fairy island which was slowly fading away in the deepening mist, that other world was slipping away from us too.

I closed my computer and never sent that update.

ABIDJAN UPHEAVAL

The president in the meantime had flown to France along with rebel leaders to work on a peace deal. The agreement signed was to let the President stay in power but to have rebel leaders be given government positions. Many Ivorians felt this was a compromise that was too costly and therefore reacted in anger. They blamed France for the results and took to the streets. People burned tires, and gunfire was heard. Others looted the city's main shopping center and radio station. Roadblocks were set up and foreigners attacked. The crowds pillaged a French school and the French cultural center. Even in the towns outside of Abidjan there were riots where churches and mosques were burned. The US embassy suggested that their people should prepare for another evacuation. In the meantime, most foreigners just stayed indoors.

POSSIBILITY OF INVASION

We got a call from Alexis on the cell phone. He told us that the rebels were planning on coming in two days' time to take over our area. He told Csaba that a rebel group sent a letter to the market town of Méagui and said that they were coming and if people joined them, all would be well. If not, they would get the "usual." Knowing what happened in other villages, the "usual" did not look like a good option, yet how could one join them? Our Bakwé colleagues and families wanted to flee into the bush like so many others had done during these invasions. Alexis called Csaba and asked him what they should do. Csaba told them to flee with their families but to take back-up discs of the translation.

When I heard this news, I got the same sort of feeling one does when standing in a beloved tract of woodland

and watching a forest fire raging your way. Why is it that when something you love is being threatened that it becomes all the more precious? All that we knew over there, a way of life, our home, the people in it, our work, were now imminently threatened. We prayed hard for them and waited to see what would happen.

NEWS

By now many of the foreigners had left the country, which caused some of the more important businesses to close including some cocoa processing plants. The country was at an impasse. President Gbagbo had successfully arranged a peace agreement to have the rebels in key posts in the government. But, the uprisings in Abidjan showed the government that the people could not tolerate the rebels controlling the interior and defense ministries as was originally planned. The rebels said that they would not renegotiate the deal. The main rebel group threatened to attack Abidjan if Gbagbo did not implement the peace accord.

In the meantime, fighting broke out again in the town of Bangolo, six hundred kilometers northwest of Abidjan. It was rumored that Liberian mercenaries allied to loyalist forces had killed many civilians in that town. By March, three rebel factions held the north and large chunks of the west. One piece of good news was that our village had not been invaded. It actually would remain safe throughout the remainder of the current upheaval.

SIGNS OF PEACE

In January of 2003 the first signs of peace were seen when both parties signed a compromise deal. President Gbagbo agreed to the deployment of neutral French and African peacekeeping forces in western Ivory Coast to rid the area of mercenaries. These troops entered the war zone to disarm the rebels and secure a cease-fire line that was agreed upon by both sides. Though some obstacles remained, it seemed that both sides of the conflict committed themselves to ending the war by signing the ceasefire. The rebels did not push any-more to hold the Ministry of the Interior or the Defense posts. The rebels now held other posts in the govern-ment. By July the country was officially out of the war. The city of Abidjan was going back to normal life and many missionaries were thinking of returning, though cautiously.

What were some of the effects of the war? Various churches in Ivory Coast experienced a greater sense of unity and growth during this conflict. One pas-tor from the Muslim north said that his church was packed as never before. We also got word that the church in our village had experienced growth. We were very relieved that the war had ended, for now. It was a weight off our minds. Yet, we knew that things would remain in an uneasy peace for a while and it would be hard to know if the country could blow up again. We had to make a decision on whether to re-turn right away or not. No one would have blamed us if we didn't return for a long time, or ever, yet, we couldn't bear the thought of the New Testament being left undone.

On the other hand, to go back right away would probably mean relocating to Mali, north of Ivory Coast. Our administration had already relocated there since they felt that Ivory Coast could remain unstable for a while still. On top of this, I was having such a hard time with this low-lying chronic fatigue that wouldn't quit, and we wondered if I could even handle going back. If we returned, all that we could see ahead was more hardship in store for us, not less, which would be difficult in my current state. We discussed what it would mean for me to go back while not in full form. I didn't want to even consider staying in the States due to my "just being tired." But what if I got worse because something else was going on underneath? That was the real issue. But what if it wasn't? I was stable enough in the States, but the traveling process would definitely wear me out.

In 2004, after talking and analyzing the situation, we decided to return in stages, resting along the way so I could recover. We'd fly into Abidjan first, and stay at our center until I was rested enough from the trip. Then we'd travel the six-hour drive to the guest house in San Pedro and rest a couple days at the ocean. Then after that, we'd drive to the village. If I could only get to the village, I was better off there because I had help with the cooking and cleaning. It was potentially very doable, and we had not received a closed door yet from the Lord. We were completely in His hands and as long as He kept the door open, even a crack, we wanted to proceed.

There was a lot to think about and nothing seemed easy for us at the moment. The only easy solution was to stay back in the States waiting for when or if Ivory Coast would be safe enough to return. In one sense a missionary is a warrior, a fighter in service for the Lord sent out by the Church. In an army, when a general gives one of his commanders a task to conquer some territory, the commander goes forth and seeks to conquer it in any way he can. If he finds that this is not possible due to barriers in his way or bad ground, he doesn't immediately quit. He tries to find new ways to accomplish his goals. And for us, as long as there was a crack in the door still open, we were going to walk through that crack until the door slammed completely shut. My health was still such that I could operate at a low level, so I wanted very badly to go back.

Then we got word from our administration that we could relocate up to Mali if we wanted to return. That way, things could settle down completely in Ivory Coast. We also got permission to fly to Ivory Coast in the fall of 2004 to visit our village for a few months, before we relocated up in Mali for the remainder of our stay. That way we could get the necessary things we needed from the village. I thought how odd it was returning now. When we left Africa two years ago, we had four children, now we were returning with only three, since Hans would be staying for college. We also would be returning to our home only as visitors and not as residents. But things change and this was a new era. At least we could see our village, if only for a few months. Maybe if things went well, we could ask permission to extend the time. We'd have to see.

In October, we flew back to Abidjan, and it felt so good to step out into the moist tropical air, to feel the sweat drip down our backs, to hear the birds we knew so well and the palm trees swaying with the breeze. It was the excitement of coming back to a place so familiar and beloved, with all the sights, sounds, and smells that Ivory Coast would never let us forget. We were met at the airport and after a bustling drive through erratic traffic, we arrived at the center. It was wonderful to see the old place that was so dear to us and held so many happy memories! After greeting our missionary family and African coworkers, we put our belongings up in the apartment, and settled in for the night.

The next day, Csaba tried to find out what the others at the center thought about the overall safety of the country. He was encouraged by what he heard. One of the missionaries who had traveled around the country, said that he had not seen any cause for concern and had rarely gotten stopped by the military. At the roadblocks they usually noticed his mission sign and would wave him on through. We also found out from others that missionariy families were starting to come back as well, which was always a good sign. Even though this was good news, this still did not mean that all was well and that something else wouldn't blow up on the horizon. Csaba asked another missionary his opinion, and he said that the country could remain in this uneasy peace for quite some time, or there could be change overnight. It was hard to know. We just prayed that when and if any change would come that it would come in a peaceful way.

Alexis, our Bakwé co-worker, came down from the village to meet us. When Csaba asked him about the safety of the roads, Alexis said they had no problems. The main roads seemed clear of highway robbers since the military were out on the roads. Perez and Firmain, our other Bakwé colleagues, came a few days later to be there for the team's yearly evaluation and planning. After the planning meetings were done, Csaba evaluated the information he had gotten from the others on the tone of the country and felt it was safe to leave for the village. But as we prepared for the trip, it still troubled me that my strength hadn't returned yet, even after some days of rest. That would be just another thing I would need to trust the Lord about.

The next day we drove to San Pedro and arrived after a five-hour trip. We drove through town and then turned down the beachfront road. When I saw the ocean against the horizon, if filled me with happy anticipation as we drove past the string of restaurants surrounded by their forest of coconut trees. This was such a happy place for us. Later, we went to the beach and it felt so good to smell the salty wind and hear the intoxicating sound of the waves beating upon the shore. I took it all in as I sat there watching the sun throw its light upon the water which scattered into a thousand sparkling gems on each dancing wave. The children were in those waves trying to catch one to ride into shore.

We planned on spending a couple nights at the guest house before heading up to the village. We were anxious to get there because we had been away for so long, over two years now. We looked forward to entering the village and being welcomed back by so many familiar people who had become so dear to us. We also longed to see our home again and get back into our routine. Yet, the day before our planned departure, something happened that would change everything. And, even though we really had tried, we never did make it back to the village that time, because another wild adventure was about to begin, one that would take us in and out of danger and across several countries.

But that is another story for another book.

THE END

ILLUSTRATION PERMISSIONS

The following illustrations were adpated with permission from photographic work by the following rightsholders:

Page 71: "African giant snail" pen and ink sketch by Noai Meyer was based on the photograph: Title: "Giant African Snail", Creator: "Ahoerstemeier" https://en.wikipedia.org/wiki/User:Ahoerstemeier/Photo_album, Source: "Giant African Snail" https://en.wikipedia.org/wiki/User:Ahoerstemeier/Photo_album, License: "CC-BY-SA" https://commons.wikimedia.org/wiki/File:Achatina_fulica_Thailand.jpg

Page 77: "Dendroaspis viridis" pen and ink sketch by Noai Meyer was based on the photograph: Title: "Western green mamba" Creator: "GlobalP" https://www.istockphoto.com/portfolio/globalp, Source: "Western green mamba" https://www.istockphoto.com/photo/western-green-mamba-dendroaspis-viridis-poisonous-white-background-gm142328093-19700986, License: "Standard" https://www.istockphoto.com/legal/license-agreement

Page 83: "Army ant" pen and ink sketch by Noai Meyer was based on the photograph: Title: "Army ant warrior", Creator: "Axel Rouvin" https://www.flickr.com/photos/39404234@N00, Source: "Army ant warrior" https://www.flickr.com/photos/39404234@N00/228545707, License: "CC BY 2.0" https://search.creativecommons.org/photos/e9fc2d71-2ed5-420e-ac6b-fa8ed709601e

Page 85: "Hen and chicks" pen and ink sketch by Noai Meyer was based on the photograph "Light Sussex bantam hen leading her week old chicks" taken by Warren Photographic, with permission to use Noai's derivative pen and ink sketch "Hen and chicks" also given by Warren Photographic, Source: "Light Sussex bantam hen leading her week-old chicks" https://www.warrenphotographic.co.uk/06716-light-sussex-bantam-hen-and-chicks

Page 116: "Bushbaby" pen and ink sketch by Noai Meyer was based on a photograph taken by Oddfeel Photography, permission to use Noai's derivative pen and ink sketch "Bushbaby" also given by Oddfeel Photography, Source: https://scontent-sjc3-1.xx.fbcdn.net/v/t1.0-9/fr/cp0/e15/q65/22049912_1736283426667320_8404160038732969074_n.jpg?_nc_cat=110&_nc_sid=110474&efg=eyJpIjoidCJ9&_nc_ohc=fbosGQDvgpIAX9yk8Dr&_nc_ht=scontent-sjc3-1.xx&tp=14&oh=8463e831e483e9ede517a5a29fbac-51d&oe=5FB2CE39